From the UN News Centre

The United Nations Association of Japan

Katsuhiko Muto

Atsumoto Ishiwata

Kazushige Cho

James Francis

Keiji Naka

Peace and Security

Economic Development

Humanitarian Aid

Environment

Human Rights

UN Affairs, Secretary-General

Women, Children, Population

Law, Crime Prevention

Health

Culture, Education

SANSHUSHA

はじめに

　「イスラム国（ISIL）」の脅威、エボラ出血熱の流行、マレーシア機の撃墜…。世界は日々、衝撃的な出来事に翻弄されています。メディアは特定の視点からそれらをセンセーショナルに報道しますが、それゆえ国連活動のような地道で堅実な活動については大きく報じられることはありません。国家、人種、民族、宗教などにおける多様な価値観が複雑に入り組む国際社会を的確に捉えるためには、公正中立である国連の活動などを通して、一方に偏らない客観的な視点を持つことはとても有益なことです。

　それと同時に、他国の出来事を「対岸の火事」として興味本位で眺めるのではなく、国際情勢を自分に身近な問題として捉え直し、自身の考えを展開させ、世界に発信していくことも極めて重要です。換言すれば、私たちに必要なのは「客観的な視点を持って主体的に国際情勢を捉える」態度と言えるでしょう。これを身につけることが本書の目的です。

　本書の各 Unit は Part A と Part B に分かれています。Part A では、UN News Centre（現・UN News）のウェブサイトの「国連ニュース（UN Daily News）」を通して、さまざまな分野の国連活動を理解することが主眼です。平和維持活動だけではない国連が行うさまざまな活動について理解を深めましょう。

　Part B では、「ジャパンタイムズ（The Japan Times）」の記事を用いて、Part A と同じトピックを別の視点から学習します。国連ニュースで紹介された国連活動を、他の機関や著者はどのように捉えているのか、またそれらが私たちの社会とどのように関係しているのかを知り、自分自身の意見やアイデアをまとめてみましょう。

　また、本書の各エクササイズは CLIL（クリル：内容言語統合型学習）という教育アプローチに基づき構成されています。英文記事を読んで理解するだけではなく、対話をリスニングする、データを分析する、記事を要約する、グループで話し合う、クラスで発表するなど、さまざまな認知的な（頭を使う）活動を通じて、英語で理解し英語で発信するための多角的なスキルを身につけることができます。

　国際情勢を「理解する」だけの時代は終わり、それについて「考えて、自ら行動する」時代が始まっています。本書がそのような時代に生きるみなさまの一助となるよう、著者一同、心から願っています。

2014 年夏
著者を代表して
武藤克彦

CONTENTS

はじめに 3
本書の構成と使い方 6
「国連ニュース」について 8

Unit 1　Peace and Security　—平和・安全保障—

Part A : 国連ニュースを読む　Security Council, senior UN officials say conflict parties must respect, protect civilians 10

Part B : The Japan Times を読む　New map shines light on Tokyo air raid horrors: Scholars record wartime history politicians would rather forget 14

Unit 2　Economic Development　—経済開発—

Part A : 国連ニュースを読む　Illicit financial outflows from Africa crippling continent's development - UN 18

Part B : The Japan Times を読む　Britain to target multinationals evading tax 22

Unit 3　Humanitarian Aid　—人道支援—

Part A : 国連ニュースを読む　Philippines: UN humanitarian chief urges donors to increase aid for typhoon recovery 26

Part B : The Japan Times を読む　North aid contingent on abductees 30

Unit 4　Environment　—環境—

Part A : 国連ニュースを読む　Former New York Mayor Bloomberg named Ban's envoy for cities and climate change 34

Part B : The Japan Times を読む　Tokyo cuts CO_2 emissions but hoards credits 38

Unit 5　Human Rights　—人権—

Part A : 国連ニュースを読む　DPR Korea human rights report elicits concern from senior UN officials 42

Part B : The Japan Times を読む　Malala's fight for girls' education 46

Unit 6 UN Affairs, Secretary-General —国連活動・国連事務総長—

Part A：国連ニュースを読む　Launching scientific advisory board, Ban urges bridging gap between science, policy 50

Part B：The Japan Times を読む　Tepco tech chief disputes Abe's "under control" assertion ... 54

Unit 7 Women, Children, Population —女性・子ども・人口—

Part A：国連ニュースを読む　Ban pledges UN commitment to advancing gender equality, women's empowerment 58

Part B：The Japan Times を読む　Hiring more women seen as answer to economic malaise: "Womenomics" pushed as fix for population woes 62

Unit 8 Law, Crime Prevention —法律・犯罪防止—

Part A：国連ニュースを読む　New UN campaign spotlights links between organized crime and counterfeit goods 66

Part B：The Japan Times を読む　Afghan opium output soars to record: UNODC 70

Unit 9 Health —健康・医療—

Part A：国連ニュースを読む　On World Diabetes Day, Ban urges greater access to healthy foods, physical activity 74

Part B：The Japan Times を読む　Veggie-heavy diet and yoga shown to slow cell aging 78

Unit 10 Culture, Education —文化・教育—

Part A：国連ニュースを読む　On International Day, UN urges support for "Mother Languages", linguistic diversity 82

Part B：The Japan Times を読む　English-language education proposal has French up in arms 86

Glossary 90

本書の構成と使い方

　本書は、UN Daily News や The Japan Times の記事を通じて、10 の分野での国際的なテーマを紹介します。1 分野につき 1Unit を割り当て、学習者が英語を使って理解を深めることができるよう、本書は CLIL の考え方に基づいて構成されています。十分に活用して、実践的な英語力を身につけましょう。本書の構成は以下のようになっています。

> ・1 Unit は Part A と Part B の 2 部構成
> ・タスクのレベルはページが進むにつれ上昇
> ・Part A と Part B のタスクはすべて 10 の Unit で共通

Part A：国連ニュースを読む

1 ページ目　記事を読む前の準備のためのページです。 Warm-up では、これから学ぶテーマについて、2 人 1 組で簡単な質問をし合って答えましょう。 Vocabulary では記事に登場するキーワードを予習します。 Dialogue では CD に収録した会話文を聞いた後、短い英文を読み、内容が合っているか (True)、間違っているのか (False) を答えてください。 Reading a News Article では記事の理解に役立つ質問を載せています。先にこの質問を読んでから、答えを探すつもりで記事を読んでみましょう。

2 ページ目　国連ニュースの記事を読みます。難しい語は太字にしていますので、Glossary（巻末の語彙リスト）で確認してください。

3 ページ目　 Reading Data では記事で学んだテーマの理解を深めるため、さまざまなデータを紹介します。データを読み込んで、要約文の空欄を埋めましょう。

4 ページ目　 Critical Analysis of Data ではリストやグラフなどを読み込んで、それらに関する自分の意見を書きます。完全な作文ではなく、空欄に意見を、書き込む形式ですので取り組みやすいはずです。 Sharing Your Opinions では書き込んだ意見を、グループに分かれて発表し合います。その際、面白いと感じた意見の内容を空欄にメモしておきましょう。

Part B: The Japan Times を読む

5ページ目 Part B では *The Japan Times* の記事を読みます。その前にまずは Listening and Taking Notes で記事の前半部分を音声で聞き、メモを取りましょう。Understanding a News Article では音声で聞いた前半部分も含め、記事全体を読みましょう。キーワードは太字で示し、巻末にまとめています。必要に応じて参照してください。

6ページ目 Understanding a News Article の2ページ目に相当します。

7ページ目 Summarizing the Article では記事の内容を要約した英文の一部が空欄になっています。単語単位ではなく、やや長めの意味の塊を入れて、要約を完成させてください。Role Play ではダイアログの一部が、空欄になっています。自分なら何をどう伝えるかを考えて、2人1組でそれぞれの話者になったつもりで会話をしましょう。

8ページ目 Discussion & Presentation ではデータを読み込み、与えられた質問について話し合ってください。By Yourself ではまずは準備として、自分の考えを表の中に書き入れましょう。次に In Your Group でグループ内で Discussion をします。書記役になった人は発言者のアイデアや意見をメモしてください。そして最後に、With the Whole Class でグループ毎の Presentation です。グループとしてまとめた内容をクラスの前で発表しましょう。

「国連ニュース」について

　本テキストのタイトルにある「国連ニュース」とは、国際連合が UN News（旧・UN News Centre）というウェブサイト（https://www.un.org/en/）上で提供しているニュースのことです。UN News は国連や国連機関の活動に関して、最新ニュース（News）だけでなく、さまざまなメディア（Video, Photo, Web TV）やジャンル（Meetings Coverage, Secretary-General）から多角的に学ぶことができる有益なサイトです。

　一般のニュースサイトと同様、トップページには主要記事や特集記事、地域別記事、ヘッドラインなどがわかりやすく配置されていますが、国連活動をある程度まとまった形で読むことができるのが「Topics」です。このセクションでは以下のような国連活動の根幹をなす各カテゴリーにおいて最新の記事が掲載されています。

Topics

Peace and Security	Women
Economic Development	Law and Crime Prevention
Humanitarian Aid	Health
Climate Change	Culture, Education
Human Rights	SDGs
UN Affairs	Migrants and Refugees

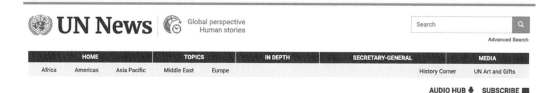

ちなみに、日本語で国連ニュースを簡潔に知りたい場合は、「国際連合広報センター」(UNIC)が日々更新している「世界の動きと国連」(https://www.unic.or.jp/news_press/world_and_un/)が便利です。ニュース以外にも、国連の基本情報や主な活動、日本で行われているイベントなど有益な情報をたくさん得ることができるので、国連英検など、国連関連の勉強をする際にはUN News Centreと併せて活用するとよいでしょう。

●写真提供

p.10	©AFP＝時事		p.50	©iStockphoto.com/MichaelUtech
p.14	© 毎日新聞社／時事通信フォト		p.54	© 時事／東北電力
p.15	© 時事／陸上自衛隊		p.58	©iStockphoto.com/LittleBee80
p.18	©EPA＝時事		p.62	© 時事通信フォト
p.22	©EPA＝時事		p.63	©iStockphoto.com/Shironosov
p.23	©AFP＝時事		p.66	© 時事
p.26	©EPA＝時事		p.70	©iStockphoto.com/mafoto
p.30	©iStockphoto.com/MarkHatfield		p.71	©AFP＝時事
p.31	© 時事		p.74	©AFP＝時事
p.34	©Imaginechina／時事通信フォト		p.78	©dpa／時事通信フォト
p.38	©AFP＝時事		p.82	©AFP＝時事
p.39	©EPA＝時事		p.86	©iStockphoto.com/takasuu
p.42	©AFP＝時事		p.87	©iStockphoto.com/richellgen
p.46	©EPA＝時事			

Peace and Security

Part A: 国連ニュースを読む

―平和・安全保障―

紛争においては多くの民間人が犠牲者となってしまう。国連安全保障理事会の役割とともに、紛争による難民を支援する方法を考えてみよう。

Warm-up Look at the picture and ask your partner, "Why are innocent people involved in a war?" 写真を見て、パートナーに "Why are innocent people involved in a war?"「なぜ罪のない人々は戦争に巻き込まれてしまうのか」と質問してみましょう。

Vocabulary Match each keyword with its definition. キーワードと意味を結びつけましょう。

(1) civilian
(2) wound
(3) residential
(4) facility
(5) embargo

- (A) to injure someone with a knife, gun, etc.
- (B) a place or building used for a particular activity or industry, or for providing a particular type of service
- (C) an official order to stop trade with another country
- (D) anyone who is not a member of the military forces or the police
- (E) containing mostly homes instead of stores, businesses, etc.

Dialogue Listen to the dialogue. Circle (T) if the statement is true or (F) if it is false. 2人の対話を聞き、内容に合っていれば (T)、違っていれば (F) に○をつけましょう。

(1) A jet fighter dropped a bomb in a housing area. (T) / (F)
(2) Sheryl can't believe the opponent's aircraft missed the targets. (T) / (F)
(3) Eddie wants all Security Council members to be more responsible. (T) / (F)

Reading a News Article With the questions below in mind, read the news article. 先に質問内容に目を通してから、記事を読みましょう。

(1) What did the Security Council and senior UN officials call for?
(2) Who is the presidency holder of the Security Council for February?
(3) What tragic event occured approximately 20 years ago?

Security Council, senior UN officials say conflict parties must respect, protect civilians

安全保障理事会、国連高官が、紛争当事国は市民の尊重と保護が義務と言明

12 February 2014 – With civilians now **routinely** targeted and **subjected to indiscriminate brutality** in most current conflicts—from the civil war in Syria to ethnic and political strife in Central African Republic (CAR) and South Sudan—the Security Council joined senior United Nations officials today to once again urge greater protection for the countless men, women and children caught in the crossfire of war.

Holding its first open debate on the topic since the release of UN Secretary-General Ban Ki-moon's most recent report, in which he notes **sombrely** that "the current state of the protection of civilians leaves little room for optimism," the Security Council sounded the alarm on behalf of desperate civilians and examined the core challenges the international community faces, from enhancing compliance with civilian protection **regimes** by non-State actors to improving humanitarian access to people in need.

A Presidential Statement adopted by the meeting reaffirmed the Council's commitment to its range of civilian protection measures initially approved in March 2002. This is the fifth edition of the Aide Memoire and is the result of consultation with the Office for the Coordination of Humanitarian Affairs (OCHA), as well as concerned UN departments and agencies, and other relevant humanitarian organizations.

The Council today also reaffirmed that Governments bear the primary responsibility to respect and ensure the human rights of citizens, and that parties to armed conflict bear the primary responsibility to **take** all **feasible steps** to ensure the protection of affected civilians.

"The Security Council stresses the need to end **impunity** for violations of international humanitarian law and **violations** and **abuses of human rights**, and reaffirms that those who have committed or are otherwise responsible for such violations and abuses must be brought to justice," according to the statement by Raimonda Murmokaité, Permanent Representative of Lithuania which holds the **rotating presidency** of the Security Council for February.

Addressing the Council, Hervé Ladsous, the Under-Secretary-General for UN Peacekeeping Operations, noted that today's debate, which comes two months ahead of the 20th anniversary of the Rwandan **genocide**, "is proof of how much has changed and how much remains the same."

More than 95 percent of peacekeepers now work in missions specifically **mandated** by the Security Council **to** protect civilians, he said, addressing the meeting which focused on effective **implementation** of protection of civilians mandates in UN peacekeeping missions, one of five core protection challenges identified by the Secretary-General.

(UN News Centre, 12 February, 2014)

Reading Data Look at the data closely and fill in the blanks in the summary. データをよく見て、要約の穴埋めをしましょう。

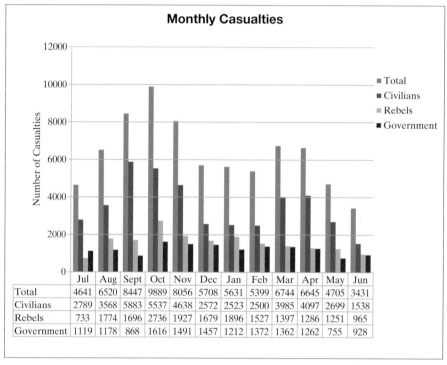

Source: The Next Century Foundation

According to the bar graph, the total number of casualties peaks in (1) _____ and bottoms out in (2) _____. For each month, the civilian casualty figure is more than that of the government or rebels. Except for July, the number of rebel victims (3) _____ that of the government in each month. In August, there are (4) _____ as many civilian victims as rebel victims. Except for the four months of December, January, (5) _____ and June, civilian casualties account for over half of the total. To sum up, it can be said that in the twelve months the number of fatalities of (6) _____ is the highest and that of government is the lowest.

Critical Analysis of Data　Examine the list and express your opinion in My opinions & ideas. リストを見て、My opinions & ideas に自分の意見を記入しましょう。

Assistance Provided by UNHCR to Refugees

- Education
- Counselling
- Mental care
- Job training
- Environmental protection
- Sanitation
- Clean water
- Shelters
- Blankets and sleeping mats
- Food
- Transportation to home
- Building a school
- Health care
- Household goods

Source: UNHCR

My opinions & ideas

Among all the items on the list, I think (1) _____

is the most urgent and critical, because (2) _____.

However, (3) _____

is not emergency assistance because (4) _____.

If I were to add another type of assistance that we could provide, it would be

(5) _____

because (6) _____.

Sharing Your Opinions　Share your opinions and ideas in your group. Write anything you find interesting about others' ideas. グループ内で自分の意見や考えについて話し合いましょう。面白いと思った他の人の意見を書きましょう。

Peace and Security

Part B: The Japan Times を読む

―平和・安全保障―

第二次世界大戦では日本でも多くの民間人が犠牲者となった。東京大空襲における被害の数を知るとともに、日本が戦争を起こす可能性について考えてみよう。

Listening and Taking Notes Listen to the first part of a news article. You can take notes while listening. ニュース記事の前半を聞きましょう。聞きながらメモをしてもよいです。

Understanding a News Article Skim the article while referring to the Glossary. 巻末の用語集を参照しつつ、記事をざっと読んで概要を把握しましょう。

New map shines light on Tokyo air raid horrors: Scholars record wartime history politicians would rather forget

新たな地図が東京大空襲の惨禍を明らかに：政治家が忘れたい戦時史を研究者が記録

In an attempt to preserve people's fading memories of the World War II **air raids** on Tokyo, scholars and citizens have drawn up what is considered the most comprehensive map so far of their efforts to escape from U.S. bombs.

In the largest air raid, the Operation Meetinghouse firebombing on March 10, 1945, an estimated 100,000 Tokyo residents, mostly civilians, were killed in a single night.

By connecting dots linking people's addresses with the places where they died, the map at the Center of the Tokyo Raids and War Damage in Koto Ward shows the directions in which they **presumably** tried to **flee**.

"We had much information from the **oral history** but few data offered a comprehensive understanding of the air raids," said Tadahito Yamamoto, a lecturer at Tokyo's Seikei University who was involved in the project.

Yamamoto said the map **validates** the **testimony** given by many survivors who say that more people died at schools and near bridges.

"We'd like to research on why the raids resulted in such a high number of victims, from the testimony and the map," he said.

The 2.5-by-2.5-meter map, titled "Great Tokyo Air Raids Life of Victims Map", was created based on data about some 10,000 people whose addresses and death locations were recorded in a **ledger** of victims.

The ledger, compiled by the Tokyo Metropolitan Government after the war, lists details on some 30,000 victims of the raids, including names, addresses, gender, location of death and where they were temporarily buried.

According to the map, 38 percent of the victims were under 19 years old and more than twice as many women between 20 and 29 died than men in that **age bracket** from the multitude of **incendiary bombs**.

In 2005, when Tokyo marked the 60th anniversary of the end of the war, museum curators and scholars drew up a similar map focused only on those killed by the catastrophic March 10 firebombing in the Shitamachi area, comprising modern-day Koto, Taito and Sumida wards, which had the highest **death tolls**.

"The Life of Victims Map" is the most comprehensive effort to visualize the overall effect of the raids because it includes those killed by raids other than Operation Meetinghouse. Over 100 air raids were carried out on the capital after November 1944.

(*The Japan Times*, March 9, 2014)

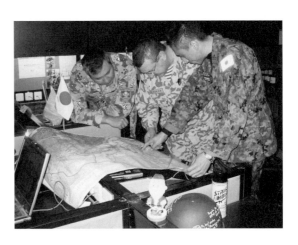

Summarizing the Article Summarize the article below. ニュース記事を以下に要約しましょう。

In an effort to preserve people's memories of the World War II air raids, a new map, the "Great Tokyo Air Raids Life of Victims Map," has been created by a group of (1) _____. A similar map from 2005 covered only the largest firebombing, "Operation Meetinghouse," which killed (2) _____. This project gives a more comprehensive view of the effects of the over 100 air raids, and is based on a ledger compiled by the Tokyo Metropolitan Government which details (3) _____ _____ of some 30,000 victims.

Role Play With your partner, take turns playing the roles of Yuta and Mika. パートナーと一緒に、Yuta と Mika の役を演じましょう。

☞ In (1), tell Yuta the reason why there are so many civilian victims.
   (1) では Yuta に、戦争において民間人の犠牲者が多い理由を述べましょう。

☞ In (2), tell Mika how to try not to be involved in a war. You can refer to Useful Expressions.
   (2) では Mika に、戦争に巻き込まれない方法を述べましょう。Useful Expressions を使ってもよいです。

[Yuta and Mika talk about war victims.]

Yuta: Did you read about the Great Tokyo Air Raids?

Mika: Yes, I was so shocked.

Yuta: Why are there always so many innocent victims in a war?

Mika: (1)_____.

Yuta: I see your point.

Mika: It's all hypothetical, but if we were in a war, how would you try to escape?

Yuta: (2)_____.

Mika: That's interesting. The mere thought of it gives me the creeps.*

*give someone the creeps: to make you feel frightened and nervous

---

💬 **Useful Expressions**

- Because S + V
- It's all / partly because S + V
- be to blame
- I would ~
- It's no use ~ing
- You cannot ~

Discussion & Presentation This is a survey on the possibility of Japan entering a war. Work in a group and discuss the question below. これは日本が戦争を起こす可能性についての意識調査です。グループで以下の質問について話し合いましょう。

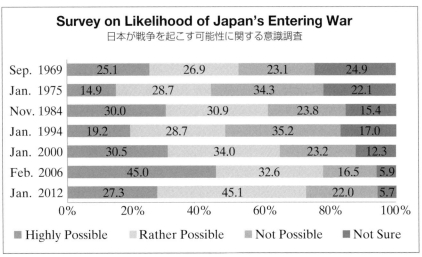

Source: 社会実情データ図録
Note: Details may not add up to total shown because of rounding.

Question How possible is it that Japan will engage in a war? 日本が今後戦争を起こす可能性は？

By Yourself Imagine the likelihood of war, the warring nation and the reason. 戦争の可能性、交戦国とその理由を想像してみましょう。

Warring nation	Likelihood	Reason
e.g., Russia	e.g., 5%	e.g., over the Northern Territories

In Your Group Discuss your ideas in a group. Someone in the group should write down all the ideas and opinions. グループ内で自分の考えを発表しましょう。グループ内の一人が全員の考えや意見をメモします。

With the Whole Class Share your group's ideas with the whole class. グループの考えをクラス全体に発表しましょう。

Name	Warring nation	Likelihood	Reason

Economic Development

Part A: 国連ニュースを読む

—経済開発—

Unit 2

発展途上国の経済開発は、国連が取り組む重要な課題のひとつだ。いまアフリカで起きている大きな問題について見てみよう。

Warm-up Look at the picture and ask your partner, "What can be done to reduce poverty in developing countries?" 写真を見て、パートナーに「発展途上国の貧困を減らすために何ができますか」と質問してみましょう。

Vocabulary Match each keyword with its definition. キーワードと意味を結びつけましょう。

(1) illicit
(2) governance
(3) capital
(4) generate
(5) multinational

- (A) the act or process of governing
- (B) to produce or cause something
- (C) having factories, offices, and business activities in many different countries
- (D) not allowed by laws or rule, or strongly disapproved of by society
- (E) money or property, especially when it is used to start a business or to produce more wealth

Dialogue (1-5 CD) Listen to the dialogue. Circle (T) if the statement is true or (F) if it is false. 2人の対話を聞き、内容に合っていれば (T)、違っていれば (F) に○をつけましょう。

(1) Eddie heard Jan's speech. (T) / (F)
(2) Africa gets less than $50 billion in official development assistance. (T) / (F)
(3) Sheryl and Eddie will likely have lots of things to do. (T) / (F)

Reading a News Article With the questions below in mind, read the news article. 先に質問内容に目を通してから、記事を読みましょう。

(1) Who is Mr. Jan Eliasson?
(2) What did Mr. Eliasson say about the figure of the money lost each year?
(3) According to Mr. Mbeki, where has all the money gone?

Illicit financial outflows from Africa crippling continent's development – UN

不正な資金流出によりアフリカ大陸の開発は妨げられている

6 February 2014 – United Nations Deputy Secretary-General Jan Eliasson and former South African President Thabo Mbeki today stressed the need for global efforts to **address** the problem of illicit financial flows from Africa, which have **crippled** the continent's development over the last few decades.

It is estimated that Africa loses over $50 billion a year in illicit financial flows, far exceeding the amount of official development assistance the continent receives.

Addressing the opening session of the High-level Panel on Illicit Financial Flows from Africa, held at UN Headquarters, Mr. Eliasson said the $50 billion in losses is a "**staggering**" figure that represents damage to individuals and Africa's development and governance agenda as a whole.

"If we can stop Africa from losing resources in illicit **outflows**, then these funds can be directed to meeting the needs of the continent's people and allowing them to build a better future," he stated.

The High-level Panel, established by the UN Economic Commission for Africa (ECA) and the African Union (AU), was **inaugurated** in February 2012 to address the **debilitating** problem of the illicit financial flows from continent. It is chaired by Mr. Mbeki and composed of nine other **distinguished** personalities from within and outside Africa.

Mr. Mbeki told a news conference after the session that the money lost each year is capital which is "generated within the continent, belongs within the continent, but then leaves by these illicit means."

About two-thirds of the illicit outflows originate from the activities of multinational corporations, while about 30 percent or so arise from "straightforward criminal activity," including **narcotics** and **human trafficking**, as well as corrupt practices.

As for where the money is going once it leaves the continent, Mr. Mbeki said the receiving countries are the developed countries as well as the tax havens.

"We've got to try and understand this matter of this illicit capital outflows out of the continent, both from the point of view of we, the exporting continent, and then the receiving countries so that our recommendations will have to address both ends of this."

The Panel is currently in the United States to meet with representatives of the US Government, private sector, academia, civil society, and multilateral institutions to discuss the issue of illicit financial flows.

It is expected to submit its final report by June this year. The report will include observations about the problem, as well as detailed proposals on how both the continent and the rest of the world can respond.

(UN News Centre, 6 February 2014)

Reading Data Look at the data closely and fill in the blanks in the summary. データをよく見て、要約の穴埋めをしましょう。

Top 10 ODA recipients in Africa
アフリカの ODA 上位10ヵ国
USD million, receipts from all donors, net ODA receipts

Ranking	Country	2010	2011	2012	Share in 2012
1	Ethiopia	3,525	3,539	3,261	6.3%
2	Dem. Rep. of Congo	3,486	5,534	2,859	5.6%
3	Tanzania	2,958	2,446	2,832	5.5%
4	Kenya	1,629	2,482	2,654	5.2%
5	Cote d'Ivoire	845	1,436	2,636	5.1%
6	Mozambique	1,952	2,085	2,097	4.1%
7	Nigeria	2,062	1,769	1,916	3.7%
8	Ghana	1,693	1,810	1,808	3.5%
9	Uganda	1,723	1,578	1,655	3.2%
10	Sudan	2,076	1,124	983	1.9%
	Other recipients	26,011	27,950	28,656	55.9%
	Total ODA recipients	47,960	51,753	51,357	100.0%

Source: OECD
Note: Details may not add up to total shown because of rounding.

The total net ODA received by African countries (1)_____ between 2010 and 2011 and slightly (2)_____ between 2011 and 2012. The Democratic Republic of Congo's share of total ODA in Africa soared between 2010 and 2011, then dropped (3)_____ between 2011 and 2012. From 2010 to 2012, while (4)_____ more than tripled its amount, (5)_____ dropped it by half. In three years top three positions have been held by Ethiopia, the Democratic Republic of Congo, Tanzania and (6)_____ . Between 2011 and 2012, (7)_____ increased by less than 1 percent.

Critical Analysis of Data Examine the list and express your opinion in My opinions & ideas. リストを見て My opinions & ideas に自分の意見を記入しましょう。

ODA to Africa by sector in 2012
As a percentage of total bilateral commitments
部門別に見たアフリカへのODA（2012年）

Sectors	World Bank(IDA*)
Education	2.8
Health	6.2
Water supply and sanitation	13.2
Government and civil society	10.2
Other social infrastructure and services	9.2
Economic	34.1
Agriculture, forestry and fishing	11.4
Trade and tourism	3.6
Humanitarian	1.7
Others	7.6
Total	100

* The International Development Association (IDA) is the part of the World Bank that helps the world's poorest countries.

My opinions & ideas

I think the World Bank does a very good job in the sector of (1) _____ because (2) _____ .
But the sector of (3) _____ needs more help from the World Bank because (4) _____
For the next 10 years, I think it is critical for Africa to develop (5) _____ much more than now and it will need less help in the sector of (6) _____ .

Sharing Your Opinions Share your opinions and ideas in your group. Write anything you find interesting about others' ideas. グループ内で自分の意見や考えについて話し合いましょう。面白いと思った他の人の意見を書きましょう。

Economic Development

Part B: The Japan Times を読む

—経済開発—

多国籍企業の極端な節税行動は、世界的規模での富の偏在に拍車をかける。英国政府のそうした企業に対する動きを見てみよう。

Listening and Taking Notes Listen to the first part of a news article. You can take notes while listening. ニュース記事の前半を聞きましょう。聞きながらメモをしてもよいです。

Understanding a News Article Skim the article while referring to the Glossary. 巻末の用語集を参照しつつ、記事をざっと読んで概要を把握しましょう。

Britain to target multinationals evading tax

多国籍企業の「節税」に英国政府が物申す

Profitable Starbucks in cross hairs for avoidance of corporate levies

LONDON – British finance chief George Osborne on Monday was expected to announce a £154 million crackdown on tax avoidance and evasion as public anger rises over the tax arrangements of big-name multinational firms.

The money, equivalent to $246.5 million, will be used to establish a team of investigators to target high-earning individuals and companies who aggressively shield their earnings from the British government.

The announcement will come a day after global coffee giant Starbucks said it was reviewing its tax affairs in Britain after it took a **roasting** from lawmakers and campaigners who accuse the chain of paying too little.

The Seattle-based firm admitted that "we need to do more," although it would not confirm a report in Britain's *Sunday Times* newspaper that it will promise this week to increase the amount of corporate tax it pays.

Under Osborne's plans, extra staffers will enable authorities to **expedite** challenges against multinationals' transfer-pricing arrangements to stop them from shifting profits out of Britain.

A new HM Revenue and Customs "center of excellence" will also be created to train staff members on tackling offshore evasion and avoidance.

It is hoped that the funding, which will be spread over two years, will result in a £2 billion ($3.2 billion) boost to tax coffers.

Starbucks had previously confirmed that it did not pay any corporate taxes in Britain for the past three years on sales worth £400 million ($640 million).

It was able to do so by paying fees to other areas of its business—such as "**royalty payments**" for the use of the brand—which resulted in the company posting a series of losses and not having to pay any corporate tax.

The *Sunday Times* said that since coming to Britain in 1998, the chain has paid just £8.6 million ($13.8 million) in corporation tax despite generating £3 billion ($4.8 billion) in revenue.

The Public Accounts Committee—a panel of British lawmakers—is due to release a report this week that is expected to criticize the measures used by corporations to avoid paying tax as the rest of the country **grapples with** tough **austerity** measures.

The committee quizzed senior figures from Starbucks, U.S. online retailer Amazon and Internet search giant Google.

"All three companies accepted that profits should be taxed in the countries where the economic activity that drives those profits takes place," the lawmakers' report said. "However, we were not convinced that their actions, in using the letter of tax laws both nationally and internationally to immorally minimize their tax **obligations**, are defensible." AFP-JIJI, AP

(*The Japan Times*, December 4, 2012)

Summarizing the Article Summarize the article below. ニュース記事を以下に要約しましょう。

LONDON – Britain announced a crackdown on tax evasion as outrage rises over the tax arrangements of multinational firms. The announcement came after Starbucks coffee confirmed that (1) _____ _____. This was done by (2) _____, resulting in the company posting a series of losses. The Public Accounts Committee —a panel of lawmakers—released a report (3) _____ _____.

Role Play With your partner, take turns playing the roles of Sam and Chris. パートナーと一緒に、Sam と Chris の役を演じましょう。

☞ In (1), tell Sam the negative aspects of charging more taxes to firms.
(1) では Sam に、企業に対してより多くの税金を課すことの悪い点について伝えましょう。

☞ In (2), tell Chris what you think about Chris' idea. You can refer to Useful Expressions.
(2) では Chris のアイデアについてどう思うかを述べましょう。Useful Expressions を使ってもよいです。

[Chris and Sam talk about paying tax.]

Chris: I think it's rational for firms to try to minimize their taxes as much as possible.

Sam: You mean as long as it's legal they have the right to do so?

Chris: Yes. I prefer less taxes and smaller government.

Sam: Well, it depends. Some big companies immorally pay less taxes in the countries where they gain huge profits.

Chris: (1)_____.

Sam: (2)_____.

💬 Useful Expressions

- It could be used for~
- You may be right but~
- Considering~
- Let me give you an example.
- It's a matter of~
- When it comes to~

Discussion & Presentation This is a table in a report made by UNICEF. Work in a group and discuss the question below. 次の表は UNICEF が作成したレポートで使われたものです。グループで以下の質問について話し合いましょう。

Poorest and Richest Countries in the World, 2007
(or latest available) in constant 2000 U.S. dollars
世界の最も貧しい国と最も豊かな国（2007年）

Poorest 10			Richest 10		
Country	GDP per capita	Population	Country	GDP per capita	Population
Dem. Rep. of Congo	94	62,522,787	Monaco	106,466	32,620
Burundi	110	7,837,981	Bermuda	72,296	64,000
Guinea-Bissau	140	1,541,040	Luxembourg	56,625	479,993
Liberia	144	3,627,285	Norway	41,901	4,709,153
Malawi	148	14,439,496	Japan	40,707	127,770,750
Eritrea	151	4,781,169	United States	38,701	301,580,000
Niger	171	14,139,684	Iceland	38,166	311,566
Ethiopia	176	78,646,128	Switzerland	37,935	7,551,117
Tajikistan	231	6,727,377	Qatar	34,960	1,137,553
Central African Rep.	231	4,257,403	Hong Kong	34,041	6,925,900

Source: UNICEF (2011)

Question What can Japan do, by cooperating with other rich countries to help those poorest countries? 日本が他の豊かな国と協力して、ここに挙げられたような最も貧しい国々に対してできることは何ですか。

By Yourself Choose one area and come up with an effective way to do it. その日本ができることについて、それをするための効果的な方法を考えましょう。

Area	How to do it
e.g., employment	e.g., tax benefits for employers hiring workers in developing countries

In Your Group Discuss your ideas with your group. Someone in the group should write down all the ideas and opinions. グループ内で自分の考えを発表しましょう。グループ内の一人が全員の考えや意見をメモします。

With the Whole Class Share your group's ideas with the whole class. グループの考えをクラス全体に発表しましょう。

Name	Area	How to do it

Humanitarian Aid

Part A：国連ニュースを読む

―人道支援―

フィリピンで起こった台風による自然災害。被災地の人々は何を必要としているのだろうか。また国連の援助は十分なのだろうか。

Warm-up Look at the picture and ask your partner, "What kinds of assistance do people in the affected area need in a natural disaster?" 写真を見て、パートナーに「自然災害のとき、被災地の人々が必要とする援助は何ですか」と質問してみましょう。

Vocabulary Match each keyword with its definition. キーワードと意味を結びつけましょう。

(1) donor
(2) relief
(3) funding
(4) restore
(5) devastate

(A) money that is provided by an organization for a particular purpose
(B) a person, group, etc. that gives something, especially money, to help an organization or country
(C) to make something return to its former state or condition
(D) to damage something very badly or completely
(E) money, food, clothes, etc. given to people who are poor or hungry

Dialogue (1-9 CD) Listen to the dialogue. Circle (T) if the statement is true or (F) if it is false. 2人の対話を聞き、内容に合っていれば (T)、違っていれば (F) に○をつけましょう。

(1) Eddie offered to help Sheryl escape from her house. (T) / (F)
(2) Sheryl is satisfied with the relief supplies she has been given. (T) / (F)
(3) Sheryl will stay in the shelter for a few more weeks. (T) / (F)

Reading a News Article With the questions below in mind, read the news article. 先に質問内容に目を通してから、記事を読みましょう。

(1) How long did it take after the typhoon hit the Philippines?
(2) In what fields is the relief aid particularly needed?
(3) As of December in 2013, how was the progress of funding the UN relief efforts?

Philippines: UN humanitarian chief urges donors to increase aid for typhoon recovery

フィリピン：国連人道担当長官、支援者に台風復興の支援増を促す

16 January 2014 – The recovery process in the Philippines has been steady but uneven, the United Nations top relief official said today, urging donors to increase support for the $788 million response plan for Filipinos, who continue to depend on humanitarian support, particularly to rebuild their homes.

"Two months after the storm, the scale and spread of humanitarian needs is still **daunting**," Under-Secretary-General for Humanitarian Affairs and Emergency Relief Coordinator Valerie Amos said in a statement from the Office of the Coordination of Humanitarian Affairs (OCHA).

"I am particularly concerned that just 20 percent of funding has been **secured** to provide tools and materials so that people can rebuild their home," she said.

The rainy season is approaching fast with flooding and landslides reported in the South-East Asia region. In the Philippines, the early rains have already led to further displacement, according to OCHA.

Urgent funding is also needed for tools and seeds so that farmers will be ready for the next planting season.

Typhoon Haiyan **swept** ashore on 8 November, killing nearly 6,000 people, **displacing** 4.1 million at the height of the emergency, and **destroying** homes and **livelihoods**.

The UN launched a one-year Strategic Response Plan for nearly $800 million in mid-December, in support of the Government's strategic plan, amounting to some $8.17 billion over four years to guide the recovery and reconstruction in the affected areas.

The plan aims to restore the economic and social conditions of the affected areas at the very least to pre-typhoon levels and to create a higher level of disaster **resilience**.

Secretary-General Ban Ki-moon saw the devastation and recovery efforts first-hand in December. Visiting Tacloban, which **bore the brunt of** the typhoon's **fury**, he told reporters that he was "deeply moved and inspired."

At the time, the overall UN **appeal** was only 30 percent funded. **Pledges** now total $331 million or around 42 percent.

"Donors, humanitarian agencies, and most of all, the people of the Philippines, have achieved a huge amount in the past two months, but the delivery and reach of aid remains uneven," Ms. Amos said in today's statement.

She noted that electricity supplies are unreliable in vast parts of the affected areas, **hampering** recovery efforts and business activities in urban areas, including Tacloban.

Many schools reopened on 6 January but there are shortages of learning spaces and school materials.

"During the next few months, the humanitarian community will focus on ensuring a smooth transition from urgent assistance to long term recovery and rehabilitation efforts," she said. "We count on the continued support of donors for this work."

(UN News Centre, 16 January, 2014)

Reading Data Look at the data closely and fill in the blanks in the summary. データをよく見て、要約の穴埋めをしましょう。

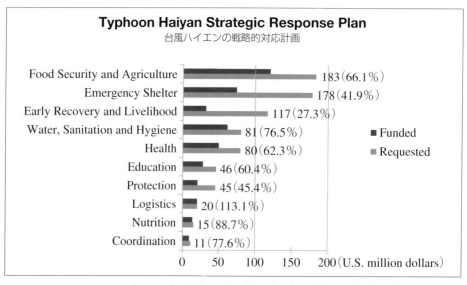

Source: the Office of the Coordination of Humanitarian Affairs (OCHA)

As of May 18, 2014, 56 percent of the total $788 million is funded. According to the graph, (1) _____ and (2) _____ are among the most required areas of support. The first one, which helps typhoon-affected people meet their immediate food needs, avoid nutritional deterioration and build food security, has secured (3) _____ percent of the initial request. The second one, also mentioned in the article, has doubled the percentage of its funding to (4) _____ percent, but its achievement rate is still low. Although (5) _____, which removes debris from public spaces and provides self-sufficiency for those who have lost their employment, is ranked after the top two, it has been the least funded of all 10 categories at (6) _____ percent.

Critical Analysis of Data Examine the list and express your opinion in My opinions & ideas. リストを見て My opinions & ideas に自分の意見を記入しましょう。

Evacuees' Possible Concerns at a Shelter

- Not Enough Supplies (food, water, clothes, and blankets)
- Health and Sanitation
- Overcrowding
- No Electricity
- Privacy
- Missed Income Opportunities
- Gender Sensitivities
- Lack of Information
- Cold Weather
- Relationships among Evacuees
- Taking Care of the Elderly or the Disabled
- Limited numbers of Staff

My opinions & ideas

Among all the items on the list, I have some ideas about (1)_____ and (2)_____. First, I'd solve (1) by (3)_____. Second, I'd solve (2) by (4)_____. However, solving (5)_____ seems difficult because (6)_____.

Sharing Your Opinions Share your opinions and ideas in your group. Write anything you find interesting about others' ideas. グループ内で自分の意見や考えについて話し合いましょう。面白いと思った他の人の意見を書きましょう。

Humanitarian Aid

Part B : The Japan Times を読む

―人道支援―

「日本人の拉致問題」と「北朝鮮への人道支援」。どちらも緊急に解決すべき問題だが、私たち日本人はどう向き合うべきか。

 Listening and Taking Notes Listen to the first part of a news article. You can take notes while listening. ニュース記事の前半を聞きましょう。聞きながらメモをしてもよいです。

Understanding a News Article Skim the article while referring to the Glossary. 巻末の用語集を参照しつつ、記事をざっと読んで概要を把握しましょう。

North aid contingent on abductees

北朝鮮への支援の前に拉致問題の解決

NEW YORK – Even if North Korea gives up its nuclear arms, Japan would not **resume** aid to the isolated state until it **clears up** the abductions of Japanese citizens dating back more than three decades, said Keiji Furuya, minister of state for the issue.

Prime Minister Shinzo Abe has intensified calls for the North to account for the **kidnappings** since he **took office** in December. His government's "firm" stance was stressed by Furuya during an international symposium in New York on Friday.

Furuya told the gathering that the abductions of at least 17 Japanese nationals during the 1970s and '80s were "acts of terrorism" by North Korea, **drawing a parallel** with the Boston Marathon bombings.

The symposium, held at the Japan Society near UN headquarters, was the second of its kind organized by the Japanese government in the United States as part of its efforts to raise global awareness of the abductees issue. The first took place in Washington the previous day.

Japan has felt particularly threatened by North Korea's recent nuclear weapons test and a long-range rocket launch in December, which resulted in tougher UN sanctions against the communist **regime**.

But Furuya said that even if the North **relents on** its weapons development, Tokyo would not help finance the huge aid projects that diplomats say Pyongyang wants and some countries are ready to consider.

"I believe it will be difficult for Japan to actively contribute to the large-scale humanitarian aid that would be resumed immediately after such developments, as long as there are no significant developments on the abduction issue," Furuya said.

He also voiced the "firm **resolution** of the nation" to uncover the fate of all the Japanese citizens **abducted** by North Korea.

In a speech at Friday's event, Maarit Kohonen Sheriff, deputy head of the New York office of the UN High Commissioner for Human Rights, expressed optimism that a new United Nations commission will contribute to resolving the abductees issue.

"It is our hope that the newly established Commission of Inquiry (will) come up with detailed analysis of such a **gross** violation of human rights by (the) DPRK, including collection and documentation of victims' testimony and account of survivors, witnesses and **perpetrators**," Sheriff said, referring to the North by its official name, the Democratic People's Republic of Korea.

In March, the UN Human Rights Council established a Commission of Inquiry to investigate human rights issues in North Korea. The number of special **rapporteurs** designated by the council has increased from one to three.

(*The Japan Times*, May 5, 2013)

> **Summarizing the Article** **Summarize the article below.** ニュース記事を以下に要約しましょう。

Since taking office, Prime Minister Abe has called on North Korea to account for the abductions of at least (1)_____ during the 1970s and '80s. At an international symposium at the Japan Society, Keiji Furuya, minister of state for the issue, called the abductions "acts of terrorism," and stressed that even if Pyongyang (2)_____, Japan would not resume aid without "significant developments on the abduction issue." The UN Human Rights Council has recently established a Commission of Inquiry focused on (3)_____ in North Korea.

> **Role Play** **With your partner, take turns playing the roles of Sam and Chris.** パートナーと一緒に、Sam と Chris の役を演じましょう。

☞ In (1), tell Sam what Japan can do to help people in North Korea.

(1) では Sam に、日本が北朝鮮の人々のために何ができるかを伝えましょう。

☞ In (2), tell Chris what you think about Chris's idea. You can refer to Useful Expressions.

(2) では Chris のアイデアについてどう思うかを述べましょう。Useful Expressions を使ってもよいです。

[Chris and Sam talk about humanitarian aid for North Korea.]

Chris: It seems nothing has been done to solve the abduction issue.

Sam: Yes. It's so frustrating, but we also need to know about the devastating situation in North Korea, where six million people are in need of assistance.

Chris: I know. A UN report says around 30 percent of children and their mothers suffer from chronic malnutrition. Can you believe this?

Sam: No, but I was wondering what Japan could do.

Chris: (1)_____.

Sam: (2)_____.

💬 Useful Expressions

- I completely agree with you.
- That's a good idea.
- I don't think so.
- I see your point, but ~
- I'm not sure if it works or not.
- I haven't thought about it.

Discussion & Presentation This is an opinion survey conducted by the Japanese government. Work in a group and discuss the question below. 次のデータは日本政府によって行われた世論調査の結果です。グループで以下の質問について話し合いましょう。

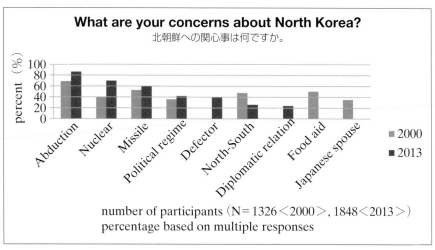

Source: 内閣府 外交に関する世論調査，2013 年 10 月

Question What is your concern about North Korea? How would you deal with it? あなたの北朝鮮への関心事は何ですか。どのようにしてその問題を解決しますか。

By Yourself Choose one area and come up with an effective way to deal with it. その関心事について考えて、解決する方法を考えましょう。

My concern	How to solve it
e.g., defector	e.g., urge China not to return them

In Your Group Discuss your ideas with your group. Someone in the group should write down all the ideas and opinions. グループ内で自分の考えを発表しましょう。グループ内の一人が全員の考えや意見をメモします。

With the Whole Class Share your group's ideas with the whole class. グループの考えをクラス全体に発表しましょう。

Name	Concern	How to solve it

Environment

Part A：国連ニュースを読む

―環境―

地球温暖化に対し国連はどういう人材をリーダーとして起用したのか。そして今後どのような計画が実施されていくのだろうか。

Warm-up Look at the picture and ask your partner, "What effects does global warming have on the environment?" 写真を見て、パートナーに「地球温暖化は環境にどのような影響を及ぼしますか」と質問してみましょう。

Vocabulary Match each keyword with its definition. キーワードと意味を結びつけましょう。

(1) emission
(2) serve
(3) address
(4) sustainable
(5) undertake

- (A) to spend a period of time doing useful work or official duties for an organization, country, important person, etc.
- (B) to start trying to solve a problem
- (C) a gas or other substance that is sent into the air
- (D) to accept that you are responsible for a piece of work, and start to do it
- (E) able to continue without causing damage to the environment

Dialogue Listen to the dialogue. Circle (T) if the statement is true or (F) if it is false. 2人の対話を聞き、内容に合っていれば(T)、違っていれば(F)に○をつけましょう。

(1) Eddie bought an ecofriendly home appliance. (T) / (F)
(2) Sheryl recommends that her co-worker use an energy-efficient vehicle. (T) / (F)
(3) Eddie wants to refrain from using his car. (T) / (F)

Reading a News Article With the questions below in mind, read the news article. 先に質問内容に目を通してから、記事を読みましょう。

(1) How long was Mr. Bloomberg mayor?
(2) Who will be attending the 2014 Climate Summit?
(3) How would Mr. Bloomberg make a city more energy efficient?

Former New York Mayor Bloomberg named Ban's envoy for cities and climate change

ブルームバーグ前ニューヨーク市長、潘事務総長の都市・気候変動担当特使に任命

31 January 2014 – Secretary-General Ban Ki-moon today announced the appointment of former New York City Mayor Michael Bloomberg as Special **Envoy** for Cities and Climate Change to **galvanize** urban action to reduce greenhouse emissions ahead of the United Nations climate summit this coming September.

"Mr. Bloomberg will assist the Secretary-General in his consultations with mayors and related key **stakeholders**, in order to raise political will and **mobilize** action among cities as part of his long-term strategy to advance efforts on climate change, including bringing concrete solutions to the 2014 Climate Summit that the Secretary-General will host in New York on 23 September 2014," the announcement said.

Mr. Bloomberg, who left office as Mayor on 31 December after 12 years in the job, currently serves as the President of the Board of the C40 Climate Leadership Group, a network of large cities from around the world committed to **implementing** meaningful and **sustainable** climate-related actions locally that will help address climate change globally.

The Secretary-General has invited leaders from Governments, businesses, finance and civil society to bring "**bold** announcements and actions" to the September summit to raise the level of ambition through new and more **robust** action on climate change. Cities play an essential role in developing and implementing actions and driving ambition, significantly affecting climate change.

Mr. Bloomberg, who served as New York City's 108th Mayor, began his career in 1966 at Salomon Brothers, a Wall Street investment bank, and launched Bloomberg LP in 1981, a financial news and information company. In 2007, Mayor Bloomberg addressed the UN Framework Convention on Climate Change in Bali, Indonesia.

In April of that year, UN Director of Sustainable Development JoAnne DiSano warmly welcomed Mr. Bloomberg's plans to reduce the **strain** on natural resources such as water, air and land by **instituting** a more energy-efficient city by rebuilding aging **water mains**, fostering greater support for **mass transit**, putting limits on vehicular **congestion** and creating more energy-efficient buildings.

"This is exactly the type of initiative that we would like more cities and communities to undertake," she said then. "Real development has to allow for economic growth and social development in an environmentally balanced way. We are strongly encouraged by this proposal."

(UN News Centre, 31 January, 2014)

Reading Data Look at the data closely and fill in the blanks in the summary. データをよく見て、要約の穴埋めをしましょう。

Total and per capita CO_2 emissions
合計および1人当たりの CO_2 排出量

Country	CO_2 emissions (2007)		
	Thousand metric tonnes of CO_2	Percentage of total CO_2	Metric tonnes of CO_2 per capita
China	6,538,367	22.30	4.96
US	5,838,381	19.91	19.38
India	1,612,362	5.50	1.43
Russian Federation	1,537,357	5.24	10.82
Japan	1,254,543	4.28	9.82
Germany	787,936	2.69	9.58
Canada	557,340	1.90	16.90
UK	539,617	1.84	8.85
Republic of Korea	503,321	1.72	10.39
Iran	495,987	1.69	6.98
World total	29,319,295	100.00	4.45

Source: Cities and Climate Change: Global Report on Human Settlements (2011)

The table shows the top 10 countries which emit the most (1)_____ (CO_2)—75 percent from the burning of fossil fuels and the remaining 25 percent mostly from deforestation. (2)_____ tops the list, emitting the most CO_2 in the world, but its emissions per capita are not as high as any other country's except (3)_____. Although (4)_____ ranks second in the total amount of CO_2, its amount per capita is the largest of all at (5)_____ metric tonnes of CO_2, which are approximately twice as much as that of the (6)_____, (7)_____, (8)_____, and the (9)_____, respectively.

(10)_____ amount per capita, the second after US, is in sharp contrast to its total release.

Critical Analysis of Data Examine the table and express your opinions in My opinions & ideas. 表を見て My opinions & ideas に自分の意見を記入しましょう。

Cities' contribution to global GHG (=Greenhouse Gas) emissions, by sector
地球温暖化ガス排出量に対する都市の分野別影響力

Sector	Percentage of global GHG emissions	Percentage of GHGs allocated to cities
Energy supply (e.g., power stations)	25.9	8.6–13.0
Industry (e.g., cement factories, oil refineries)	19.4	7.8–11.6
Forestry	17.4	0
Agriculture	13.5	0
Transport (e.g., private motor vehicles)	13.1	7.9–9.2
Residential and commercial buildings (e.g., heating and lighting)	7.9	4.7–5.5
Waste and waste water (e.g., landfill methane)	2.8	1.5
Total	100	30.5–40.8

Source: Cities and Climate Change: Global Report on Human Settlements (2011)

My opinions & ideas

If I were the mayor of (1) _____ (a city's name), I would first focus on the sector of (2) _____ because (3) _____.

There are a number of ways to address the problem, but I would (4) _____.

On the other hand, I wouldn't tackle the sector of (5) _____ because (6) _____.

Sharing Your Opinions Share your opinions and ideas in your group. Write anything you find interesting about others' ideas. グループ内で自分の意見や考えについて話し合いましょう。面白いと思った他の人の意見を書きましょう。

Environment

Part B: The Japan Times を読む

—環境—

東京が始めた温暖化対策は効果を上げているのだろうか。CO_2 の削減状況とその要因、そして今後の課題を確認しておこう。

Listening and Taking Notes Listen to the first part of a news article. You can take notes while listening. ニュース記事の前半を聞きましょう。聞きながらメモをしてもよいです。

Notes

Understanding a News Article Skim the article while referring to the Glossary. 巻末の用語集を参照しつつ、記事をざっと読んで概要を把握しましょう。

Tokyo cuts CO_2 emissions but hoards credits

東京、CO_2 排出を削減するも排出権は温存

About four years after Asia's first **mandatory** greenhouse gas emissions-reduction scheme was launched by the Tokyo Metropolitan Government, businesses in the capital have succeeded in drastically cutting carbon dioxide emissions without depending on emissions credit trading.

Due mainly to the March 2011 Fukushima nuclear crisis, which reduced utilities' electricity supplies and **triggered** legal **curbs** on power consumption by **large-lot** customers that year, Tokyo offices and factories covered by the **cap-and-trade** system have been able to easily meet their carbon dioxide reduction targets, a metropolitan government official said.

The program, which started in April 2010, caps energy-related emissions of around 1,400 offices, commercial buildings and factories that consume more than 1,500 kiloliters of energy in crude oil equivalent terms and allows for trading of emissions credits earned via reductions of more than obligatory levels.

In the first phase, lasting from fiscal 2010 to 2014, such offices and factories are required to **trim** total carbon dioxide emissions by 6 to 8 percent from base-year levels. In the fiscal 2015-2019 second phase, the reduction must be 15 to 17 percent. Factories face less **stringent** targets than offices.

Base-year levels were calculated from average emissions over three **consecutive** years between fiscal 2002 and 2007.

The program was introduced to help Tokyo, which consumes around the same amount of energy as entire Northern European countries like Norway, achieve its goal of **slashing** carbon dioxide and other heat-trapping gas emissions by 25 percent by 2020 compared with 2000 levels.

So far, more than 90 percent of offices and factories covered by the system have achieved the 6 to 8 percent targets, and 70 percent of the facilities have already met the 15 to 17 percent goals, said Yuki Arata, director of the metropolitan government's emissions cap-and-trade section.

In fiscal 2012, which ended on March 31, 2013, offices and factories covered by the scheme achieved a 22 percent reduction in emissions compared with their base-year levels.

As of last December, emissions credit transactions in Tokyo only **amounted to** 22 cases, with most of the businesses covered by the scheme believed to **retain** credits earned through their own emissions-cutting efforts.

"Emissions credit transactions have so far been inactive as many businesses have managed to sharply slash emissions on their own," Arata said. "Those who want to sell the credits to secure funding for future energy-saving investments are still monitoring the situation."

(*The Japan Times*, March 14, 2014)

Summarizing the Article Summarize the article below. ニュース記事を以下に要約しましょう。

Four years after the start of a mandatory greenhouse gas emissions-reduction plan, Tokyo businesses have drastically cut carbon dioxide emissions without (1)____ _____. The "cap-and-trade" system yields credits that may be sold for future energy-saving investments. The goal of this program is to cut carbon dioxide and other gas emissions by 25 percent compared with 2000 levels. Due mainly to (2) _____, which reduced electricity supplies and led to other conservation measures, around 1,400 offices, commercial buildings and factories have achieved (3) _____ _____.

Role Play With your partner, take turns playing the roles of Sam and Chris. パートナーと一緒に、Sam と Chris の役を演じましょう。

☞ In (1), tell Sam whether Japan should restart the nuclear power plants.
(1) では Sam に、日本が原子力発電所を再開すべきかどうかを述べましょう。

☞ In (2), tell Chris what you think about Chris's idea. You can refer to Useful Expressions.
(2) では Chris のアイデアについてどう思うかを述べましょう。Useful Expressions を使ってもよいです。

[Chris and Sam talk about energy resources in Japan.]

Chris: Since the Fukushima crisis, Japan has been dependent on thermal power generation.

Sam: Yes. Now almost 90 percent of their energy comes from coal, oil and LNG.

Chris: And they haven't used nuclear energy ever since.

Sam: That's right. But some people say that Japan should restart its nuclear power plants because they emit no CO_2. What do you think?

Chris: (1)_____.

Sam: (2)_____.

💬 Useful Expressions

- I agree.
- That sounds good.
- What do you mean?
- Do you think it's possible?
- I doubt it.
- That's unreasonable.

Discussion & Presentation This is a graph on reduction targets and GHG emissions in major countries. Work in a group and discuss the question below. 次のデータは主要国の削減目標と温室効果ガス排出状況についてのグラフです。グループで以下の質問について話し合いましょう。

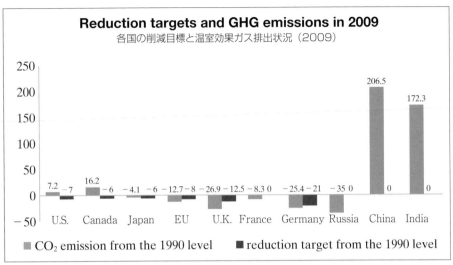

Source: 環境省　STOP THE 温暖化 2012

Question What can Japan do to meet its reduction target? 日本は削減目標を達成するために何ができますか。

By Yourself Think of a way to solve global warming. 地球温暖化を解決する方法を考えましょう。

Field	How to solve it
e.g., education	e.g., teach children how to save energy

In Your Group Discuss your ideas with your group. Someone in the group should write down all the ideas and opinions. グループ内で自分の考えを発表しましょう。グループ内の一人が全員の考えや意見をメモします。

With the Whole Class Share your group's ideas with the whole class. グループの考えをクラス全体に発表しましょう。

Name	Field	How to solve it

Human Rights

Part A: 国連ニュースを読む

—人権—

世界にはいまだに人権が抑圧され、非人道的な行為が横行している国もある。ここでは北朝鮮における人権問題について見てみよう。

Warm-up Look at the picture and ask your partner, "What human rights do you know about?" 写真を見て、パートナーに「あなたの知っている人権にはどんなものがありますか」と質問してみましょう。

Vocabulary Match each keyword with its definition. キーワードと意味を結びつけましょう。

(1) extermination
(2) enslavement
(3) imprisonment
(4) abortion
(5) persecution

- (A) state of being in prison, or the time someone spends there
- (B) the act of treating someone cruelly or unfairly over a period of time, especially because of their religious or political beliefs
- (C) a medical operation to end a pregnancy so that the baby is not born alive
- (D) the act of making someone a slave
- (E) the act of killing large number of people or animals of a particular type so that they no longer exist

Dialogue Listen to the dialogue. Circle (T) if it is true or (F) if it is false. 2人の対話を聞き、内容に合っていれば (T)、違っていれば (F) に○をつけましょう。

(1) Eddie hasn't read the report about human rights in North Korea. (T) / (F)
(2) Sheryl thinks the situation in North Korea is a trifling matter. (T) / (F)
(3) Sheryl thinks the UN alone could influence the supreme leader of North Korea.
(T) / (F)

Reading a News Article With the questions below in mind, read the news article. 先に質問内容に目を通してから、記事を読みましょう。

(1) Who is the supreme leader of North Korea now?
(2) What is Mr. Ban seriously concerned about?
(3) What does ICC stands for?

DPR Korea human rights report elicits concern from senior UN officials

人道に対する罪が横行する北朝鮮に、国連幹部が強い懸念

18 February 2014 – Secretary-General Ban Ki-moon and United Nations High Commissioner for Human Rights, Navi Pillay, today urged the Democratic People's Republic of Korea (DPRK) to engage with the international community to improve its human rights record after a UN-mandated report catalogued **crimes against humanity** of an "unimaginable scale" being committed in the country.

Mr. Ban is seriously concerned about human rights and the **humanitarian** situation in the DPRK, his spokesperson said in a statement. As such, the Secretary-General remains "deeply disturbed" by the findings.

Noting that human rights are universal values, he "hopes the report will contribute to raising international awareness about grave violations of those values in [the country]," the statement said.

In a separate statement, the UN High Commissioner for Human Rights Navi Pillay said that since January 2013, she has urged the international community to put much more effort into tackling the human rights situation of people in DPRK.

"It has now published a historic report, which sheds light on violations of a terrifying scale, the **gravity** and nature of which—in the report's own words—do not have any **parallel** in the contemporary world."

The report, released yesterday and which will be formally presented to the Human Rights Council in Geneva on 17 March, documents crimes such as "extermination, murder, enslavement, torture, imprisonment, rape, forced abortions and other sexual violence, persecution on political, religious, racial and gender grounds, forcible transfer of **populations**, enforced disappearance and the inhumane act of knowingly causing prolonged starvation."

In her reaction, Ms. Pillay suggested that the international community has paid "insufficient attention" to these human rights violations which have been ongoing.

"That has now been partly **rectified**," she noted but called for strong international leadership to follow up on the Commission's finding and "to use all the mechanisms at its disposal to ensure accountability, including referral to the International Criminal Court (ICC)."

In addition to the report, the Commission included a copy of a letter sent to Supreme Leader Kim Jong-un, containing a summary of the systematic, widespread and gross human rights violations that "entail crimes against humanity."

The letter states that the three-member panel would recommend referral of the situation in the DPRK to the ICC "to render accountable all those, including possibly yourself, who may be responsible for the crimes against humanity referred to in this letter and in the Commission's report."

(UN News Centre, 18 February, 2014)

Reading Data Look at the data closely and fill in the blanks in the summary. データをよく見て、要約の穴埋めをしましょう。

Worst 10 countries for death sentences and executions in 2013
死刑判決と執行数の最も多い10ヵ国（2013年）

Ranking	Country	Executions	Death sentences
1	Iran	369*	91
2	Iraq	169*	35
3	Saudi Arabia	79*	6*
4	United States of America	39	80
5	Somalia	34*	117*
6	Sudan	21*	29*
7	Yemen	13*	3*
8	Japan	8	5
9	Vietnam	7*	148*
10	Taiwan	6	7
	Others	33	1400*
	Total	778	1921

(*: at least)
Source: Amnesty International

In 2013, (1) _____ 778 people were executed in the world. According to Amnesty International, thousands of people were put to death in China in 2013, but the figure is not included in the total. China and North Korea keep this data a state secret. About (2) _____ percent of all known executions were recorded in the top two countries: Iran and (3) _____. Saudi Arabia executed at least (4) _____ people. Although Maryland became the 18th state to abolish the death penalty, (5) _____ became fourth in the ranking. Japan became (6) _____ among the countries in East Asia, followed by (7) _____ and Taiwan.

Critical Analysis of Data Examine the list and express your opinion in My opinions & ideas. リストを見て My opinions & ideas に自分の意見を記入しましょう。

Types of Harassment or Discrimination
ハラスメントや差別のタイプ

Types	Examples
Sexual	unwanted touching, sexual insults, staring
Racial	racist comments on his/her skin color, language, national origin
Sexual Orientation	intentionally exposing his/her sexual orientation
Religious	attacks on his/her religious beliefs
Disability	insulting based on a physical or mental disability
Social or Economic class, Family status	name calling such as "welfare mother," "trailer trash"
Personal Appearance	calling him/her "ugly," taunting him/her because of their height or weight

Reference: Sexual Harassment & Assault Response & Education / Mount Allison University

My opinions & ideas

I think (1) _____ harassment is more pervasive than any other types of harassment in Japan now because (2) _____ .
On the other hand I find (3) _____ harassment is very rare because (4) _____ .
If I am harassed and suffer for it then it might result in (5) _____ . I don't think the situation will change overnight but we need to (6) _____ .

Sharing Your Opinions Share your opinions and ideas in your group. Write anything you find interesting about others' ideas. グループ内で自分の意見や考えについて話し合いましょう。面白いと思った他の人の意見を書きましょう。

Human Rights

Part B: The Japan Times を読む

―人権―

世界にはまだ、女性が教育を受ける機会を奪われている国がある。女性が教育を受ける権利を命がけで訴えて、2014年にノーベル賞を受賞したマララさんの言葉を聞いてみよう。

 Listening and Taking Notes Listen to the first part of a news article. You can take notes while listening. ニュース記事の前半を聞きましょう。聞きながらメモをしてもよいです。

Notes

Understanding a News Article Skim the article while referring to the Glossary. 巻末の用語集を参照しつつ、記事をざっと読んで概要を把握しましょう。

Malala's fight for girls' education
女性が教育を受ける権利のための、マララさんの戦い

Malala Yousafzai, the Pakistani campaigner for girls' education who survived an **assassination** attempt by the Taliban last year, has been awarded the Sakharov Prize for Freedom of Thought by the European Parliament. We congratulate Malala and welcome the award as an effort to promote schooling for the huge number of children worldwide who are **deprived of** education opportunities.

In her speech at the Nov. 20 award ceremony in Strasbourg, France, Malala pointed to the **plight** of as many as 57 million children around the world who are denied opportunities to go to school. Those children "do not want an iPhone, a PlayStation or chocolate. They just want a book and a pen," she said.

She urged the Western world to see beyond their borders "to the suffering countries where people are still deprived of their basic rights, their freedom of thought is **suppressed**, freedom of speech is **enchained**." Many children in those countries "have no food to eat, no water to drink, and children are starving for education," she said.

Malala, who fought against a Taliban ban on education for girls in her native town in the Swat District of Pakistan, was shot in the head and neck by Taliban gunmen while she was returning from school in October 2012. She recovered from the near-fatal assault in Britain, where she was flown for treatment. She resettled there with her family and now campaigns for girls' education.

In her address to the United Nations in July, she stressed the importance of education to support countries suffering from terrorism. Instead of sending weapons and tanks to those countries, send books and pens, she said.

Despite the global **acclaim** for her activities that have won her many other international awards on human rights, Malala's achievements have not been welcomed by everybody in her native Pakistan. Her detractors reportedly charge that Malala is being used in a campaign to emphasize the negative aspects of the country, including terrorism, or that the Western show of respect for her heroic activism is an act of **hypocrisy** that ignores the suffering of many civilian victims of U.S. **drone** strikes in Pakistan. Pakistani private schools have banned Malala's **autobiography** *I Am Malala*, published in October, from their libraries because of its "anti-Pakistan and anti-Islam content."

According to UNESCO, Pakistan has the world's second highest number of children out of school—5.1 million in 2010—and girls make up two-thirds of these children. The situation is most **dire** in rural areas, where education for girls is all too often opposed on religious grounds. We urge Islamabad to strive to ensure that all Pakistani children have an opportunity to receive an education.

(*The Japan Times*, December 3, 2013)

Summarizing the Article Summarize the article below. ニュース記事を以下に要約しましょう。

　Malala Yousafzai, the Pakistani campaigner for girls' education who survived a Taliban assassination attempt, has been awarded the Sakharov Prize for Freedom of Thought by the European Parliament. In her acceptance speech (1) _____ _____. Malala's achievements, however, (2) _____ _____. Detractors charge that (3) _____. Pakistan has the world's second highest number of children out of school—5.1 million—and two-thirds of these children are girls.

Role Play With your partner, take turns playing the roles of Sam and Chris. パートナーと一緒に、Sam と Chris の役を演じましょう。

☞ In (1), tell Sam something you can do to stop harassment.
(1) では Sam に、ハラスメントを阻止するためにできることを伝えましょう。

☞ In (2), tell Chris another thing you can do to stop harassment. You can refer to Useful Expressions.
(2) では Chris が述べたこと以外で、ハラスメントを阻止するためにできることを述べましょう。Useful Expressions を使ってもよいです。

[Chris and Sam talk about sexual harassment.]

Chris: Nearly half of 7th to 12th graders experienced sexual harassment in the previous school year, according to a study in 2011.

Sam: That's a very serious situation. Where did they do the research?

Chris: Believe it or not, it was done in the United States.

Sam: Oh, no! It can't be! What can we do to stop it?

Chris: (1)_____.

Sam: (2)_____.

💬 Useful Expressions

- If I were a school teacher I would ~
- Another good thing would be to ~
- I agree with you and ~
- It's critically important to ~
- In addition to ~

Discussion & Presentation This is a chart based on statistics from WHOA, a volunteer organization in the US fighting online harassment. Work in a group and discuss the question below. 次のグラフはインターネットでのハラスメントと戦うアメリカのボランティア団体の統計を基に作成したグラフです。グループで以下の質問について話し合いましょう。

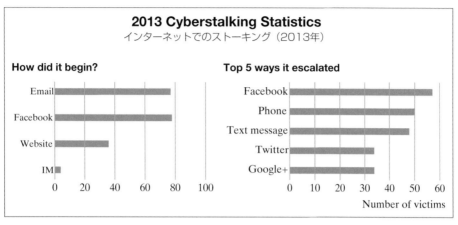

Source: WHOA

Question What would be an effective precaution to prevent online harassment?
インターネット上のハラスメントに遭わないようにするための、効果的な予防策にはどんなことがあるでしょうか。

By Yourself Come up with an effective way to prevent it. 効果的な予防策を考えてみましょう。

How to prevent it
e.g., avoid sharing personal information

In Your Group Discuss your ideas with your group. Someone in the group should write down all the ideas and opinions. グループ内で自分の考えを発表しましょう。グループ内の一人が全員の考えや意見をメモします。

With the Whole Class Share your group's ideas with the whole class. グループの考えをクラス全体に発表しましょう。

Name	How to prevent it

UN Affairs, Secretary-General

Part A: 国連ニュースを読む

―国連活動・国連事務総長―

持続可能な環境を築くには、政策だけでなく科学技術が果たす役割も重要である。地球温暖化を例に、同様に不可欠な個人としてできることについても考えてみよう。

Warm-up Look at the picture and ask your partner, "What's happening?" 写真を見て、パートナーに "What's happening?"「何が起きているのですか」と質問してみましょう。

Vocabulary Match each keyword with its definition. キーワードと意味を結びつけましょう。

(1) authorities
(2) policy-making
(3) press conference
(4) sustainable
(5) prosperity

- (A) a meeting in which a public figure gives information to news reporters and answer questions
- (B) the act or process of creating laws or setting standards for a government or business
- (C) when people have money and everything that is needed for a good life
- (D) the people or organizations that are in charge of a particular country or area
- (E) able to continue without causing damage to the environment

2-1 CD

Dialogue Listen to the dialogue. Circle (T) if the statement is true or (F) if it is false.
2人の対話を聞き、内容に合っていれば (T)、違っていれば (F) に○をつけましょう。

(1) Sheryl watched today's press conference. (T) / (F)
(2) Eddie believes private is more important than public. (T) / (F)
(3) Sheryl thinks that sustainable technology is necessary. (T) / (F)

Reading a News Article With the questions below in mind, read the news article. 先に質問内容に目を通してから、記事を読みましょう。

(1) Where was the inaugural meeting of the Scientific Advisory Board held?
(2) What will Mr. Ban preside over at UN Headquarters on 23 September?
(3) What will Mr. Ban confirm in the 50th Munich Security Conference?

Launching scientific advisory board,
Ban urges bridging gap between science, policy

潘事務総長が科学諮問委員会を設置、科学と政策の溝埋めを促す

30 January 2014 – The United Nations must use science and technology to strengthen its **policy-making** on **sustainable** development, reducing inequality and **eradicating** extreme poverty, Secretary-General Ban Ki-moon today said launching his advisory board of scientists.

"For too long we have sought to burn and consume our way to prosperity. That model is unsustainable," Mr. Ban said in remarks at the **inaugural meeting** of the Scientific Advisory Board in Berlin.

Composed of 26 **eminent** scientists in varied natural, social and human **disciplines**, the Board is meant to strengthen ties between the UN and the global scientific community so that science can be more effectively integrated in policy-making processes.

"We have entered a new era, which has been given the name 'Anthropocene,'" he said, referring to a newly coined term for the current **geologic epoch** defined by humans' impact on the planet.

"We need science to understand our environment, to protect it and use it wisely," he noted, adding that science is also needed to **tackle** hunger and food security, growing inequalities, disaster prevention, **urbanization, sanitation** and sustainable energy for all.

The launch of the Board, whose Secretariat is within the UN Educational, Scientific and Cultural Organization (UNESCO), comes as Mr. Ban is pushing to **catalyse** action and strengthen political will towards a global legal climate agreement by the end of 2015.

Ahead of those discussions, Mr. Ban will host a climate summit on 23 September at UN Headquarters in New York for global leaders from Government, business, finance, and civil society.

Environmental sustainability is one of the eight anti-poverty targets known as the Millennium Development Goals (MDGs). The international community is currently in the 700 day countdown to the deadline for achieving those targets and amidst defining a post-2015 development **agenda**.

While in Germany, Mr. Ban will address the 50th Munich Security Conference where he will stress that global security ultimately depends on sustainable development.

Earlier today, he met with Interior Minister Thomas de Maizière, Economic and Cooperation Development Minister Gerd Müller, and Foreign Minister Frank-

Walter Steinmeier.

In a press conference alongside Mr. Steinmeier, the Secretary-General **highlighted** Germany's role in the peaceful settlement of disputes, peacebuilding and **disarmament**, enhancing respect for human rights, and support for international development efforts.

He is also due to meet with Federal President Joachim Gauck and Federal Chancellor Angela Merkel.

He will travel to Bonn tomorrow to meet with UN staff members and local authorities.

(UN News Centre, 30 January, 2014)

Reading Data Look at the data closely and fill in the blanks in the summary. データをよく見て、要約の穴埋めをしましょう。

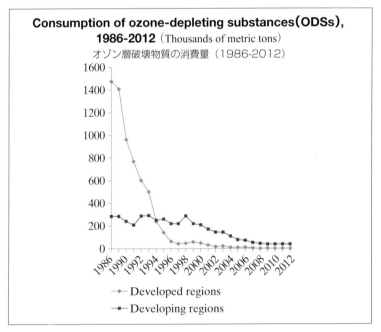

Source: The Millennium Development Goals Report 2014

According to the line graph, in 1986, the amount of the consumption of ODSs in developed regions was about (1) _____ as much as that in developing regions. The amount of ODSs in developed regions keeps (2) _____ sharply for the span of 10 years, and in (3) _____ it becomes the same as that of developing regions. It keeps falling until 1996 and fluctuates, becoming virtually zero toward 2012. The transition in the amount of ODSs in developing regions shows a completely different pattern. Beginning with the amount of 300 thousands metric tons, it (4) _____ between 1986 and 1998. It gradually (5) _____ from 2000 to (6) _____, showing no obvious change after that.

Critical Analysis of Data Examine the list and express your opinion in My opinions & ideas. リストを見て、My opinions & ideas に自分の意見を記入しましょう。

9 Ways to Reduce Global Warming

- Use less heat and air conditioning
- Replace plastic water bottles with a reusable one
- Change a light bulb
- Buy energy-efficient products
- Use less hot water
- Use the "off" switch
- Choose to buy local products
- Plant a tree
- Encourage others to conserve

My opinions & ideas

Among the 9 ways on the list, I think (1)_____

is the easiest to do, because (2) _____ .

However, (3) _____

is a little difficult to do because (4) _____ .

If I were to add another way to reduce global warming, it would be (5)_____

because (6) _____ .

Sharing Your Opinions Share your opinions and ideas in your group. Write anything you find interesting about others' ideas. グループ内で自分の意見や考えについて話し合いましょう。面白いと思った他の人の意見を書きましょう。

UN Affairs, Secretary-General

Part B: The Japan Times を読む

―国連活動・国連事務総長―

原発の現状において、時として政府と専門家の考えは異なる。オリンピックに向けた原発の現状や、未来の代替エネルギーについて考えてみよう。

Listening and Taking Notes Listen to the first part of a news article. You can take notes while listening. ニュース記事の前半を聞きましょう。聞きながらメモをしてもよいです。

Understanding a News Article Skim the article while referring to the Glossary. 巻末の用語集を参照しつつ、記事をざっと読んで概要を把握しましょう。

Tepco tech chief disputes Abe's "under control" assertion
東電技術顧問、安倍首相の「制御」言明に異議

A Tokyo Electric Power Co. executive **created a stir** Friday by stating that he doesn't believe the **radioactive** water leaks at the Fukushima No. 1 plant are under control—**contradicting** Prime Minister Shinzo Abe's bold assertions in Tokyo's Olympics presentation in Buenos Aires.

During the Tokyo bid team's appeal for the 2020 Games on Sept. 7, Abe assured the International Olympic Committee that "the situation is under control" and "the effects from the **contaminated** water have been perfectly blocked within the (artificial) bay" of the wrecked nuclear complex.

At a meeting Friday in Koriyama, Fukushima Prefecture, however, Kazuhiko Yamashita, Tepco's top technology executive, **reportedly** told Democratic Party of Japan lawmakers that he "does not believe (Tepco) is able to control" the situation.

Later in the day, Tepco released a press release claiming Yamashita was only talking about some unexpected leaks at some of the hundreds of water tanks and other troubles at the **compound**, and that only the seawater in the utility's artificial bay had been affected.

"In that sense, we share the same understanding as that of the prime minister," Tepco executive and spokesman Masayuki Ono said at Friday's press conference at the utility's headquarters.

By saying "the situation is under control," Abe and Tepco meant to say that the densities of the radioactive **contaminants** in seawater outside that bay are far below their legal limits, Ono said.

In the meantime, Ono admitted that the water in the artificial bay is being constantly refreshed by the ocean, which presumably allows radioactive contaminants to be swept out to sea.

Some experts say the radiation densities are being kept low by dilution rather than any steps by Tepco to "control" the flow of contaminated leaks and groundwater into the sea.

Asked about this view, Ono argued that Tepco has made various efforts to control the situation, including measures to keep the melted fuel in the damaged **reactors** cool.

Despite the fact that emergency cooling measures are the sole cause of all the radioactive water leaving the plant, Ono gave Tepco's "measures" credit for keeping the density of the radioactive elements entering the seawater low outside the bay.

(*The Japan Times*, September 13, 2013)

Summarizing the Article Summarize the article below. ニュース記事を以下に要約しましょう。

Tepco's top technology executive, Kazuhiko Yamashita, (1) _____ by stating that he "does not believe Tepco is able to control" the radioactive water leaks at the Fukushima No. 1 plant—contradicting Prime Minister Shinzo Abe's assertions in (2) _____ _____. Abe had assured the International Olympic Committee that "the situation is under control." Later, Tepco (3) _____ _____ claiming Yamashita was only talking about some unexpected leaks at some of the hundreds of water tanks and other troubles at the compound, and that only the seawater in the utility's artificial bay had been affected.

Role Play With your partner, take turns playing the roles of Nao and Shinji. パートナーと一緒に、Nao と shinji の役を演じましょう。

☞ In (1), tell Nao why Prime Minister Abe said so.
   (1) では Nao に、安倍首相がそのように述べた理由を伝えましょう。

☞ In (2), tell Shinji how the situation in Fukushima nuclear plant is now. You can refer to Useful Expressions.
   (2) では Shinji に、福島原子力発電所の現状について、専門家がどのように述べているか伝えましょう。Useful Expressions を使ってもよいです。

[Nao and Shinji talk about the Prime Minister's presentation.]

Nao: Do you remember that Prime Minister Abe stressed the safety of the Fukushima nuclear plants in Tokyo's Olympics presentation?

Shinji: Yes, I do. But some people back then thought it was too soon to say that.

Nao: Right. Why do you think he had to say that?

Shinji: (1)_____.

Nao: I agree with you. That's why Japan is going to host the next Olympics.

Shinji: What do experts say about the current situation in Fukushima?

Nao: (2)_____.

Shinji: Oh, really. I didn't know that. We should all keep a sharp lookout for* it.

*keep a sharp lookout for: to watch with special attention for

---

💬 Useful Expressions

- I think it's because ~
- According to the newspaper [Internet], ~
- I heard that ~
- They say ~
- I'm not sure, but I ~
- Rumor has it that ~

Discussion & Presentation This is the percentage of electricity generated by various fuel types in 2010 and an energy forecast for 2030. Work in a group and discuss the question below. これは2010年と2030年に計画されている燃料別の発電源の割合です。グループで以下の質問について話し合いましょう。

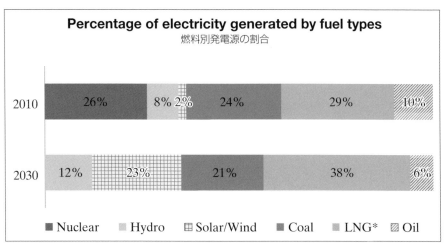

*LNG = liquid natural gas
Source: TOMIC
Note: Details may not add up to total shown because of rounding.

Question What are the best three fuel types? 最良の発電燃料を3つ選ぶとすれば、どれだと思いますか。

By Yourself Choose three fuel types and think about their advantages and disadvantages.
発電源を3つ選び、その利点と欠点を考えましょう。

Fuel type	Advantages	Disadvantages
e.g., coal	e.g., low cost	e.g., more CO_2 emissions

In Your Group Pick the best fuel and discuss your ideas with your group. Someone in the group should write down all the ideas and opinions. 最良の発電源を1つ選び、グループ内で自分の考えを発表しましょう。グループ内の一人が全員の考えや意見をメモします。

With the Whole Class Share your group's ideas with the whole class. グループの考えをクラス全体に発表しましょう。

Name	Best fuel	Advantages	Disadvantages

Women, Children, Population

Part A: 国連ニュースを読む

—女性・子ども・人口—

女性の人権尊重、地位向上が叫ばれてから久しい。世界の女性就業率を考えるとともに、Gender-neutral words（性的に中立な語）についても学習しよう。

Warm-up Look at the picture and ask your partner, "What do you think is happening?"

写真を見て、パートナーに "What do you think is happening?"「何が起きていると思いますか」と質問してみましょう。

Vocabulary Match each keyword with its definition. キーワードと意味を結びつけましょう。

(1) crucial
(2) discrimination
(3) empower
(4) root for ~
(5) equality

- (A) to give a person or organization the legal right to do something
- (B) take sides with; show strong sympathy for
- (C) extremely important or significant
- (D) a situation in which people have the same rights, advantages, etc.
- (E) the practice of treating one person or group differently from another in an unfair way

Dialogue Listen to the dialogue. Circle (T) if the statement is true or (F) if it is false.

2人の対話を聞き、内容に合っていれば (T)、違っていれば (F) に○をつけましょう。

(1) Eddie does not agree with Mr. Ban's statement.　(T) / (F)
(2) Sheryl thinks women are supposed to behave in a certain way in Japan.　(T) / (F)
(3) Eddie believes that equality is no longer crucial.　(T) / (F)

Reading a News Article With the questions below in mind, read the news article. 先に質問内容に目を通してから、記事を読みましょう。

(1) What is UN Women for?
(2) When was the Beijing World Conference on Women held?
(3) What did Mr. Ban say about the 2014 Winter Olympic Games?

Ban pledges UN commitment to advancing gender equality, women's empowerment

潘事務総長、性の平等と女性の地位向上の進展に国連の関与を誓約

4 February 2014 – Secretary-General Ban Ki-moon today pledged to root for women everywhere ahead of his departure for the Winter Olympics in Sochi, while stressing the need for the United Nations and its partners to **lay the groundwork** to enable all women to enjoy their rights and be **empowered**.

"We are at a key moment," Mr. Ban said at a **photo-op** with former United States Secretary of State Hillary Clinton and Phumzile Mlambo-Ngcuka, the Executive Director of the UN Entity for Gender Equality and the Empowerment of Women (UN Women), ahead of their meeting at UN Headquarters.

He noted that 2015 will be **crucial** for the future of development and the future of women's rights. Next year marks the target date for the achievement of the global anti-poverty targets known as **the Millennium Development Goals**, which contain specific benchmarks for gender equality.

Countries are also working toward the adoption of global development agenda beyond 2015, as well as on securing a global climate change agreement by the end of next year.

2015 also marks the 20th anniversary of the **landmark** Beijing World Conference on Women. **The Beijing Declaration and the Platform for Action**, adopted **unanimously** by 189 countries, is considered the key global policy document on gender equality, addressing critical areas such as women and poverty, violence against women and the human rights of women.

"There has been a great deal of progress since then, but too many women still face far too much discrimination and violence," said Mr. Ban, adding that the UN family looks forward to continuing to work closely with Ms. Clinton for sustainable development and opportunities for all the world's women and girls.

The UN chief is set to leave New York today for Russia, where he will attend the opening ceremony on Friday of the 2014 Olympic Winter Games.

The Games, he said, show the power of sport to unite people regardless of gender or **sexual orientation**. This year's Games will also **showcase** progress for women, who will be competing for the first time in the ski jump.

This week UN Women is hosting a number of events on gender equality **on the margins of** the current meeting of the working group tasked with preparing a proposal on the Sustainable Development Goals called for by Member States at the 2012 UN Conference on Sustainable Development, held in Rio de Janeiro, Brazil.

Gender equality and women's empowerment are among the overall issues being discussed by the group, along with oceans and seas, forests, **biodiversity**, conflict prevention, post-conflict peacebuilding and the promotion of durable peace, and rule of law and governance and promoting equality.

(UN News Centre, 4 February, 2014)

Reading Data Look at the data closely and fill in the blanks in the summary.
データをよく見て、要約の穴埋めをしましょう。

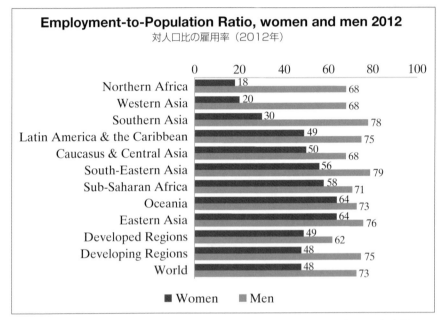

Source: UN Women

According to the bar graph, the ratio of women's employment-to-population in the world to that of men's is 48 to (1) _____. Compared to developed regions, the difference between women and men in developing regions is (2) _____. Among the (3) _____ parts of the world, the gap between women and men is the biggest in (4) _____. (5) _____ , where Japan is located, has the smallest gap between genders. All in all, it is patently obvious that no part of the world has a (6) _____ employment rate of women than men.

Critical Analysis of Data Examine the list and express your opinion in My opinions & ideas. リストを見て、My opinions & ideas に自分の意見を記入しましょう。

Gender-neutral Words
性的に中立な語

It is important to be aware of the need to use language that will not offend anyone on the basis of gender. Here are some examples of gender-neutral words.

Not Preferable	Preferable
actress	actor
stewardess	flight attendant
businessman	businessperson
cameraman	camera operator
career woman	career professional
fireman	fire fighter
heroine	hero
hostess	host
maid	house cleaner
master	expert
waitress	server

My opinions & ideas

Among the word pairs on the list, I think the pair (1) _____

and _____ is the easiest to understand because (2) _____.

However, the pair (3) _____ and _____

is a little funny because (4) _____ .

In Japanese, I think (5) _____ is the gender-neutral word

for (6) _____ .

Sharing Your Opinions Share your opinions and ideas in your group. Write anything you find interesting about other's ideas. グループ内で自分の意見や考えについて話し合いましょう。面白いと思った他の人の意見を書きましょう。

Women, Children, Population

Part B: The Japan Times を読む

―女性・子ども・人口―

日本の人口減少が止まらない。女性が仕事上で抱えるストレスを参考に、日本における Womenomics（女性が作り出す経済）の今後を考えてみよう。

Listening and Taking Notes Listen to the first part of a news article. You can take notes while listening. ニュース記事の前半を聞きましょう。聞きながらメモをしてもよいです。

Understanding a News Article Skim the article while referring to the Glossary. 巻末の用語集を参照しつつ、記事をざっと読んで概要を把握しましょう。

Hiring more women seen as answer to economic malaise: "Womenomics" pushed as fix for population woes

女性雇用増が景気低迷の打開策か：人口問題対策として推される「ウーマノミクス」

Imagine our current discussions about women and the workplace—Can women have it all? How do women lean in?—taking place in a country with one of the worst gender-equality ratios in the world.

This is Japan. And women, it turns out, could be key to **jolting** the nation out of its **economic coma**.

Japan's population is **shrinking** faster than anywhere else in the world. The government estimates the population will fall by roughly 15 percent, or 20 million people, by 2040. With this steep drop, the tax base and labor force will **plummet**, all while state spending on the elderly rises, creating a long-term economic crisis.

One solution? More babies. In 2007, the health minister referred to women as "birth-giving machines" and **implored** them "to do their best per head." This year, one female Diet member, Seiko Noda, proposed that **abortions** be banned to boost population numbers.

Others point to the **boardroom**, citing economic arguments that bringing women into the labor force would be more immediately helpful to the nation's fortunes.

Even Prime Minister Shinzo Abe is leaning into this bedroom-versus-boardroom debate.

Abe has promoted women's workforce potential as part of his broader plan for economic revival. His challenge is great: Japan has fallen into **recession** three times since 2008, and government debt—at more than 200 percent of gross domestic product—is the highest on the planet.

"It's possible that Japan's **stagnation** is essentially men's fault," Abe said in a recent speech. "The period in which men with **uniform** ways of thinking dominated Japan's business community was too long… The mission that I have imposed upon myself is to thoroughly liberate the power that women possess."

Kathy Matsui, the chief Japan equity strategist at Goldman Sachs, has published reports for more than a decade on "**womenomics**" in Japan.

Her research estimates the nation could add 8.2 million people to its labor force and lift GDP by up to 15 percent by closing the gender gap. The employment rate is currently 60 percent for women versus 80 percent for men.

Organizations and firms from the World Economic Forum to McKinsey & Company Inc. have released similar findings showing that women's increased participation would be the single most effective way to improve Japan's growth prospects.

A study by the Center for Work-Life Policy found that 74 percent of college-educated women in Japan **go "off-ramp,"** more than double the U.S. figure.

"We are sort of wasting half the population," said Yoko Ishikura, a professor of business strategy at Keio University. "If I were a 15-year-old girl in Japan, I would get out of the country."

(*The Japan Times*, September 18, 2013)

Summarizing the Article Summarize the article below. ニュース記事を以下に要約しましょう。

Japan's population is shrinking. Estimates predict a drop of 15 percent, or (1) _____, by 2040. With this, the tax base and labor force will plummet, while spending on the elderly rises, creating a long-term economic crisis. Prime Minister Shinzo Abe has promoted women's (2) _____, or "womenomics," as part of his plan for economic revival. The current employment rate is 60 percent for women versus 80 percent for men. Organizations such as the World Economic Forum have released findings showing that women's increased participation would be the most effective way to (3) _____.

Role Play With your partner, take turns playing the roles of Daiki and Rio. パートナーと一緒に、Daiki と Rio の役を演じましょう。

☞ In (1), tell Rio why she can choose comprehensive work.

(1) では Rio に、女性が総合職を選んでもよい理由を伝えましょう。

☞ In (2), tell Daiki what he should do in the workplace. You can refer to Useful Expressions.

(2) では Daiki に、女性が多い職場ですべきことを教えてあげましょう。Useful Expressions を使ってもよいです。

[Daiki and Rio talk about job hunting.]

Daiki: How is your job hunting coming along*?

Rio: I'm still thinking I should choose clerical work because I'm a woman.

Daiki: You can do comprehensive work if you want because (1)_____
_____.

Rio: Oh, really? Maybe I shouldn't be so stereotypical. So how about you?

Daiki: I'm thinking about working at an insurance company, but the problem is there are usually lots of women working in insurance companies.

Rio: Then you should (2)_____.

Daiki: Thanks for your advice.

Rio: You're welcome. You should remember the word "womenomics," Daiki.

*come along: to make progress

💬 Useful Expressions

- I think ~
- in my opinion ~
- I doubt ~
- be careful about ~
- be aware of ~
- try to ~

Discussion & Presentation This is a part of a survey conducted on full-time female office workers. Work in a group and discuss the question below. これは正社員として勤務する女性社員に行った調査結果の一部です。グループで以下の質問について話し合いましょう。

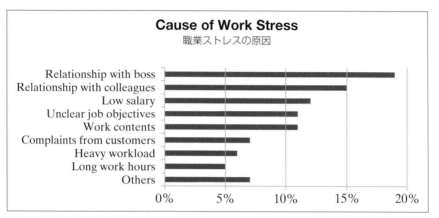

Source: エン ウィメンズワーク

Question If you were an office worker, what would you do to help female workers relieve their stress? もしあなたが会社員だったら、どのようにして女性社員がストレスを減らす手助けをしますか。

By Yourself Choose two causes of stress from above and think about how you could help them. 上からストレスの原因を2つ選び、その解決方法を考えましょう。

Cause of stress	How you help
e.g., heavy workload	e.g., help them with their work

In Your Group Pick one cause of stress and its solution and share them in your group. Someone in the group should write down all the ideas and opinions. ストレスの原因と解決策を1つ選び、グループ内で自分の考えを発表しましょう。グループ内の一人が全員の考えや意見をメモします。

With the Whole Class Share your group's ideas with the whole class. グループの考えをクラス全体に発表しましょう。

Name	Cause of stress	Solution

Law, Crime Prevention

Part A：国連ニュースを読む

―法律・犯罪防止―

一部の国で起きているように見えて、実際には国際社会に大きな影響を与える犯罪もある。ここでは偽造品を巡る問題を見ていこう。

Warm-up Look at the picture and ask your partner, "What do you think is the most critical crime the world has to prevent?" 写真を見て、パートナーに「国際社会が防止に取り組むべき、最も重大な犯罪は何だと思いますか」と質問してみましょう。

Vocabulary Match each keyword with its definition. キーワードと意味を結びつけましょう。

(1) counterfeit ・
(2) laundering ・
(3) fraud ・
(4) trafficking ・
(5) exploitation ・

・ (A) the act of transferring money, so that illegal receipts are made to appear legitimate
・ (B) the buying and selling of illegal good, especially drugs
・ (C) treating someone unfairly to benefit from their work
・ (D) the crime of deceiving people
・ (E) made to look exactly like something else, in order to deceive people

Dialogue Listen to the dialogue. Circle (T) if the statement is true or (F) if it is false.
2人の対話を聞き、内容に合っていれば (T)、違っていれば (F) に○をつけましょう。

(1) Sheryl went to some Asian countries to check on the situation of counterfeiting. (T) / (F)

(2) Sheryl thinks the problem is under control in those countries and emphasized the bright side of the situation. (T) / (F)

(3) In the fight against counterfeiting, Eddie thinks the local governments do their jobs right. (T) / (F)

Reading a News Article With the questions below in mind, read the news article. 先に質問内容に目を通してから、記事を読みましょう。

(1) What does UNODC stands for?

(2) According to UNODC, what can counterfeit products lead to?

(3) Which is a lower-risk/higher-profit opportunity for criminals, drug trafficking or counterfeiting?

New UN campaign spotlights links between organized crime and counterfeit goods

国連の新キャンペーンが告発する、組織犯罪と偽造品ビジネス

14 January 2014 – The United Nations today launched a new campaign to raise awareness about the links between organized crime and the trade in counterfeit goods, which amounts to $250 billion a year.

The campaign—"Counterfeit: Don't buy into organized crime"—informs consumers that buying counterfeit goods could be funding organized criminal groups, putting consumer health and safety at risk and contributing to other **ethical** and environmental concerns.

Launched by the Vienna-based UN Office on Drugs and Crime (UNODC), the campaign centres around a new public service announcement which will be featured on the NASDAQ screen in New York's Times Square today and aired on several global television stations from January.

Through the campaign, consumers are urged to look beyond counterfeit goods and to understand the serious **repercussions** of this illicit trade, which provides criminals with a significant source of income and facilitates the laundering of other illicit **proceeds**.

"As a crime which touches virtually everyone in one way or another, counterfeit goods pose a serious risk to consumer health and safety," UNODC states in a news release. "With no legal regulation and very little **recourse**, consumers are exposed to risk from unsafe and ineffective products since **faulty** counterfeit goods can lead to injury and, in some cases, death."

Tyres, brake pads and airbags, aeroplane parts, electrical consumer goods, baby formula and children's toys are just some of the many different items which have been counterfeited, according to UNODC.

Fraudulent medicines also present a serious health risk to consumers, the agency pointed out. Criminal activity in this area is big business: the sale of fraudulent medicines from East Asia and the Pacific to South-East Asia and Africa alone amounts to some $5 billion per year.

The list of fraudulent medicines is extensive, and can range from ordinary painkillers and **antihistamines**, to "lifestyle" medicines, such as those taken for weight loss and sexual dysfunction, to life-saving medicines including those for the treatment of cancer and heart disease.

"In comparison to other crimes such as drug trafficking, the production and distribution of counterfeit goods present a low-risk/high-profit opportunity for criminals," noted UNODC Executive Director Yury Fedotov.

"Counterfeiting feeds money laundering activities and encourages corruption. There is also evidence of some involvement or overlap with drug trafficking and other serious crimes," he said.

UNODC also noted that counterfeiting involves a range of ethical issues that are often overlooked, including labour exploitation and migrant **smuggling**, as well as poses environmental challenges due to the lack of any regulations.

（UN News Centre, 14 January, 2014）

Reading Data Look at the data closely and fill in the blanks in the summary. データをよく見て、要約の穴埋めをしましょう。

Intellectual Property Rights Seizures Statistics in Fiscal Year 2013
知的財産権に関する押収の統計（2013 年度）

FY 2013 Source Economy	Estimated MSRP	Percent of Total
China	1,180,919,064	68%
Hong Kong	437,538,041	25%
India	20,683,669	1%
Korea	6,308,434	Less than 1%
Singapore	5,065,398	Less than 1%
Vietnam	4,406,367	Less than 1%
Taiwan	3,975,422	Less than 1%
Great Britian	2,421,034	Less than 1%
Bangladesh	1,914,318	Less than 1%
Pakistan	1,335,728	Less than 1%
All other economies	78,948,105	5%
Total FY 2013 Est. MSRP*	**1,743,515,580**	
Number of seizures	**24,361**	

Source: Economies by MSRP*

FY 2013 Commodity	Estimated MSRP	Percent of Total
Handbags/Wallets	700,177,456	40%
Watches/Jewelry	502,836,275	29%
Consumer electronics/Parts	145,866,526	8%
Wearing apparel/Accessories	116,150,041	7%
Pharmaceuticals/Personal care	79,636,801	5%
Footwear	54,886,032	3%
Other	143,962,451	8%
Total FY 2013 Est. MSRP	**1,743,515,582**	
Number of seizures	**24,361**	

Commodities by MSRP
* Manufacturer's Suggested Retail Price
Source: U.S. Department of Homeland Security
(US $)

According to Intellectual Property Rights Seizures Statistics in Fiscal Year 2013 from the U.S. Department of Homeland Security, (1) _____ was the dominant supplier of counterfeit products to the U.S., which accounts for (2) _____ percent. Next comes (3) _____ at (4) _____ percent. (5) _____ out of the top 10 countries in the list are in Asia. The average manufacturer's suggested retail price is (6) _____ dollars. Based on the MSRP of the genuine versions of the counterfeit commodities, the four most valuable imitations were of handbags and wallets, watches and jewelry, which together account for (7) _____ percent of about 1.7 billion dollars in total.

Critical Analysis of Data Examine the list and express your opinion in My opinions & ideas. リストを見て、My opinions & ideas に自分の意見を記入しましょう。

Nature of threat of counterfeit consumer products
消費財の偽造品がもたらす脅威の種類

1.	Dangerous goods for sale	no – or poor quality – controls (e.g., fake baby food; dangerous toys; tainted milk)
2.	Exploitative working conditions	dangerous unregulated sweatshops
3.	Linkages to other TOC*	TOC groups distributing counterfeits are often associated with other crime types, e.g., prostitution, money laundering, human trafficking.
4.	Lost government revenues	loss of import duties; loss of sales tax; lower renenues overall
5.	Facilitates corruption	undermines rule of law and accountability

* Transnational Organized Crime

Reference: Transnational Organized Crime in East Asia and the Pacific: A Threat Assessment, April 2013 by UNODC

My opinions & ideas

I think (1) _____ is the most critical to Japan because (2) _____.

From the global point of view, (3) _____ would be the clear and imminent danger we should address first because (4) _____.

In order to tackle those threats, I think it is very important to (5) _____ and (6) _____.

Sharing Your Opinions Share your opinions and ideas in your group. Write anything you find interesting about others' ideas. グループ内で自分の意見や考えについて話し合いましょう。面白いと思った他の人の意見を書きましょう。

Unit 8: Law, Crime Prevention

Part B: The Japan Times を読む

―法律・犯罪防止―

麻薬を撲滅するためには、需要と供給の両方の面からの取り組みが必要です。ここでは、アフガニスタンを舞台にしたアヘンの供給に関する問題を見ていきましょう。

2-11 CD **Listening and Taking Notes** Listen to the first part of a news article. You can take notes while listening. ニュース記事の前半を聞きましょう。聞きながらメモをしてもよいです。

Notes

2-12 CD **Understanding a News Article** Skim the article while referring to the Glossary. 巻末の用語集を参照しつつ、記事をざっと読んで概要を把握しましょう。

Afghan opium output soars to record: UNODC

アフガニスタンでアヘンの生産が急増中

JALALABAD, AFGHANISTAN – Afghanistan's **opium** production surged this year to record levels, despite international efforts over the past decade to **wean** the country **off** the **narcotics** trade, according to a report released Wednesday by the UN's drug control agency.

The harvest this past May resulted in a staggering 5,500 metric tons of opium, 49 percent higher than last year and more than the combined output of the rest of the world. Even Afghan provinces with some past successes in combating **poppy** cultivation saw those trends reversed, according to this year's annual UN Office on Drugs and Crime report.

The withdrawal of foreign troops from Afghanistan next year is likely to make matters even worse, said Jean-Luc Lemahieu, the UNODC regional representative in Kabul. He warned that as international assistance falls off, the Afghan government will become increasingly reliant on illicit sources of income. Uncertainty is also driving up poppy production, as farmers worried about the country's future turn to the **tried and true**.

The big increase in production began in 2010 when farmers rushed to plant to take advantage of soaring prices, a result of a crop disease the previous year, the U.S. military surge in the south and the announcement of the U.S. and NATO's transition out of Afghanistan, Lemahieu told AP.

Lemahieu said those who benefit from the drug trade include farmers, **insurgents** and many within the government. Often, he said, they work together.

Past attempts by the international community to combat opium cultivation have included introducing alternative crops and paying farmers in some areas not to plant poppies. That **backfired** when farmers elsewhere started growing poppies in the hopes of getting money if they stopped.

Cultivation also appears to be spreading to new parts of the country—with Afghans planting poppies in some 209,000 hectares across 17 provinces this year, compared with 154,000 hectares in 15 provinces in 2012, according to the report.

But it wasn't all bad news in the report, which said Afghanistan has expanded its social services to deal with a growing **addiction** problem at home.

"These are **tangible** and hopeful signs of improvement," the report said.

There are roughly 1 million drug addicts in Afghanistan, 15 percent of whom are women and children, said Kanishka Turkistan, spokesman for the ministry of public health.

(*The Japan Times*, March 1, 2013)

Summarizing the Article Summarize the article below. ニュース記事を以下に要約しましょう。

JALALABAD, AFGHANISTAN – Despite international efforts in Afghanistan, (1) _____. Jean-Luc Lemahieu, the UNODC regional representative in Kabul, said that (2) _____ _____, as the Afghan government will become increasingly reliant on illicit sources of income. Past attempts to fight opium cultivation have included the introduction of alternative crops and payments to not grow poppies. The report also noted, among "tangible and hopeful signs of improvement," that (3) _____.

Role Play With your partner, take turns playing the roles of Sam and Chris. パートナーと一緒に、Sam と Chris の役を演じましょう。

☞ In (1), tell Sam the reason why uncertainty causes the increase of opium production..

(1) では Sam に、先に読んだ記事を参考にして、将来が不確実だと、なぜアヘンの生産量が増えるのか、その理由を伝えましょう。

☞ In (2), tell Chris what caused the uncertainty. You can refer to Useful Expressions.

(2) では何がそういった状況を招いたのか、自分で考えた理由を伝えましょう。Useful Expressions を使ってもよいです。

[Chris and Sam talk about Afghanistan's opium production.]

Chris: Why has Afghanistan's opium production surged?

Sam: For one thing, it's a matter of supply and demand. In 2009, the supply dropped because of a crop disease. That led to soaring prices, and farmers rushed to plant the next year.

Chris: I would add that uncertainty also causes the increase.

Sam: Why is that?

Chris: (1)_____.

I wonder what caused the uncertainty.

Sam: (2)_____.

💬 Useful Expressions

- Suppose ~
- make the same old mistake
- It might be a wishful thinking but ~
- What would you do?
- One reason would be ~
- What would happen to ~?

Discussion & Presentation This is a chart based on statistics from UNODC. Work in a group and discuss the question below. 次の表は UNODC 作成の統計に基づいたものです。グループで以下の質問について話し合いましょう。

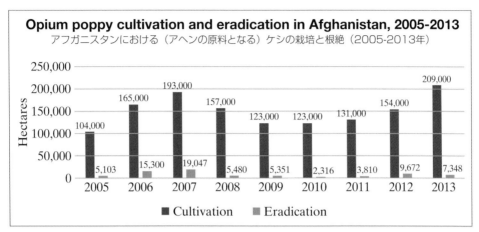

Source: UNODC World Drug Report 2014

Question Why did Afghanistan's opium production surge from 2011? What can we do to curb the trend? アフガニスタンのアヘンの生産が 2011 年から急増したのはなぜですか。この傾向にストップをかけるために、私たちにできることは何でしょうか。

By Yourself Come up with an effective way to address the problem. この問題に取り組むための効果的な方法を考えてみましょう。

The effective way
e.g., help farmers increase and stabilize their income

In Your Group Discuss your ideas with your group. Someone in the group should write down all the ideas and opinions. グループ内で自分の考えを発表しましょう。グループ内の一人が全員の考えや意見をメモします。

With the Whole Class Share your group's ideas with the whole class. グループの考えをクラス全体に発表しましょう。

Name	Field	How to address it

Health Part A：国連ニュースを読む

Unit 9

―健康・医療―

国連は糖尿病対策に健康食品や運動を推奨している。世界の患者数はどのくらいだろうか。糖尿病を予防するにはどんな方法があるだろうか。

Warm-up Look at the picture and ask your partner, "How much do you care about your diet?" 写真を見て、パートナーに "How much do you care about your diet?"「どのように食生活に気をつけていますか」と質問してみましょう。

Vocabulary Match each keyword with its definition. キーワードと意味を結びつけましょう。

(1) obesity
(2) diabetes
(3) diet
(4) diagnosis
(5) treatment

- (A) a serious disease in which there is too much sugar in the blood
- (B) something that is done to cure someone who is injured or ill
- (C) when someone is very fat in a way that is unhealthy
- (D) the kind of food that a person or animal eats each day
- (E) the process of discovering exactly what is wrong with someone or something through close examination

Dialogue (2-13 CD) Listen to the dialogue. Circle (T) if the statement is true or (F) if it is false. 2人の対話を聞き、内容に合っていれば (T)、違っていれば (F) に○をつけましょう。

(1) Eddie is not so happy with the results of his health checkup.　　(T) / (F)
(2) Sheryl recommends that young people go on a diet.　　(T) / (F)
(3) Sheryl suggests that Eddie use a home exercise machine.　　(T) / (F)

Reading a News Article With the questions below in mind, read the news article. 先に質問内容に目を通してから、記事を読みましょう。

(1) What did Ban request countries and communities to do in terms of food production?
(2) To what extent is the number of people with diabetes expected to increase in 2030?
(3) What does WHO state about the great majority of people with diabetes?

On World Diabetes Day, Ban urges greater access to healthy foods, physical activity

世界糖尿病デーに潘事務総長がさらなる健康食品や運動の活用を要請

14 November 2013 — Secretary-General Ban Ki-moon today urged lowering the number of people living with **diabetes**—increasingly younger and poorer—by changing unhealthy lifestyles that include poor diets and a lack of exercise.

"In today's **world of plenty**, it is shameful that so many people lack access to healthy foods," Mr. Ban stated in his message for World Diabetes Day, observed annually on 14 November.

Instead of relying on fast foods and quick solutions, he called on countries and communities "to support **smallholder** and family farmers, foster sustainable agriculture and encourage people to eat healthful **produce** and support physical activity."

Approximately 350 million people are currently living with diabetes and the number is expected to double between 2005 and 2030, according to **projections** by the UN World Health Organization (WHO).

Earlier this year, countries meeting at the World Health Assembly adopted a Global Action Plan for the Prevention and Control of Noncommunicable Diseases calling on countries to stop the rise in **obesity** and the associated rise in diabetes.

"On World Diabetes Day, I call on Governments to make good on their commitments to address **non-communicable diseases**, including by fostering sustainable food production and consumption," Mr. Ban said, "and I encourage all people to minimize their personal risk."

Diabetes—which occurs when the **pancreas** does not produce enough insulin, or when the body cannot effectively use the **insulin** it produces—has become one of the major causes of **premature illness** and death in most countries, mainly through the increased risk of **cardiovascular disease** (CVD).

More than 80 percent of people with diabetes live in low- and middle-income countries and are frequently between 35 and 64 years old, WHO reported, adding that early **diagnosis** and proper treatment are key to controlling the disease.

"Nearly one hundred years after insulin was first used to save the life of a diabetic patient, people around the world still die because they cannot access this hormone," Mr. Ban stated.

Started by WHO and the International Diabetes Federation (IDF), the Day is celebrated on 14 November to mark the birthday of Frederick Banting who, along with Charles Best, was **instrumental** in the discovery of insulin in 1922, a life-saving treatment for diabetes patients.

(UN News Centre, 14 November, 2013)

Reading Data Look at the data closely and fill in the blanks in the summary. データを見て、要約の穴埋めをしましょう。

Countries with the highest numbers of estimated cases of diabetes for 2000 and 2030
糖尿病の推定患者数が最も多い国（2000年と2030年）

Ranking	2000		2030	
	Country	People with diabetes (millions)	Country	People with diabetes (millions)
1	India	31.7	India	79.4
2	China	20.8	China	42.3
3	USA	17.7	USA	30.3
4	Indonesia	8.4	Indonesia	21.3
5	Japan	6.8	Pakistan	13.9
6	Pakistan	5.2	Brazil	11.3
7	Russian Federation	4.6	Bangladesh	11.1
8	Brazil	4.6	Japan	8.9
9	Italy	4.3	Philippines	7.8
10	Bangladesh	3.2	Egypt	6.7

Source: American Diabetes Association

Looking at the table, we can see the sheer numbers of people in the world who are afflicted. This table, however, provides pure (1)_____ not percentages, of people with diabetes, so it might over-represent the disease in highly-populated countries like (2)_____ and China. The order of the top (3)_____ countries remain the same in 2030 but the numbers are expected to double in each country. In 2000, the Russian Federation and Italy are ranked in the top 10, but the Philippines and (4)_____ enter the 2030 ranking instead. Although Japan ranks fifth in 2000 and (5)_____ in 2030, the number of patients is expected to (6)_____ by about 30 percent.

Critical Analysis of Data Examine the list and express your opinion in My opinions & ideas. リストを見て、My opinions & ideas に自分の意見を記入しましょう。

Tips to Lose Weight

- Keep a food journal
- Drink 6 cups of water a day
- Eat more greens
- Cook with fat free broth
- Eat whole grains
- Measure everything
- Take your time eating
- Use smaller plates
- Exercise
- Eat more seafood
- Use meat as a condiment
- Eat more fiber
- Eat more vegetarian meals
- Eat healthy snacks

My opinions & ideas

Among all the items on the list, I think (1)_____

is the most effective way to lose weight, because (2)_____.

However, I'm skeptical about (3)_____,

because (4)_____.

If I were to add one way to lose weight, I would recommend (5)_____,

because (6)_____.

Sharing Your Opinions Share your opinions and ideas in your group. Write anything you find interesting about others' ideas. グループ内で自分の意見や考えについて話し合いましょう。面白いと思った他の人の意見を書きましょう。

Health Part B: The Japan Times を読む

—健康・医療—

老化を防止するには野菜やヨガなどが有効であるとされる。一方、老化の原因に挙げられるストレスは、どのように軽減すべきだろうか。

 Listening and Taking Notes Listen to the first part of a news article. You can take notes while listening. ニュース記事の前半を聞きましょう。聞きながらメモをしてもよいです。

Understanding a News Article Skim the article while referring to the Glossary. 巻末の用語集を参照しつつ、記事をざっと読んで概要を把握しましょう。

Veggie-heavy diet and yoga shown to slow cell aging
野菜の多い食生活とヨガが細胞の老化を防止

LONDON — The fountain of youth may simply be a healthy diet and reduced stress after all, not a magic pill or expensive cosmetics.

Comprehensive lifestyle changes, including more fruit and vegetables as well as **meditation** and yoga, were shown to reverse signs of aging at the **cellular** level for the first time in a study published Sept. 16.

Adopting a diet rich in unprocessed foods combined with moderate exercise and stress management over five years increased the length of **telomeres**, the ends of **chromosomes** linked to aging, according to a study of 35 men published in the Lancet medical journal. No previous study has shown the effect of lifestyle changes on telomere length, the authors said.

The research, led by Dean Ornish, founder of the San Francisco-based **Preventive Medicine** Research Institute, adds to evidence of the benefits of healthy habits. Ornish's "Lifestyle Heart Trial," published in 1998, showed a reversal of **coronary** heart disease over five years. Patients who receive 72 hours of training from medical professionals on Ornish's program for reversing heart disease have been **reimbursed** by Medicare since January 2011.

"So often, people think it has to be a new drug or laser, something really hightech and expensive, to be powerful," Ornish said in a telephone interview. "Our studies are showing that simple changes in our lifestyle have powerful impacts in ways that we can measure."

Ornish collaborated on the study with Elizabeth Blackburn, who shared the Nobel Prize in medicine in 2009 with Carol Greider and Jack Szostak for research on the telomerase "**immortality enzyme**," which prevents telomeres from being shaved off.

He was inspired by Blackburn's research showing that the shortening of telomeres, and therefore aging, is accelerated by emotional stress such as that experienced by women who have parents with Alzheimer's disease or children with **autism**.

"My general experience is that things in biology go both ways," said Ornish, a professor of medicine at the University of California, San Francisco. "If bad things make them shorter, maybe good things make them longer. So we had lunch together and I said, 'Why don't we find out?'"

The study included 35 men with low-risk **prostate cancer** enrolled between 2003 and 2007. Ten men adopted the lifestyle changes, while 25 underwent active **surveillance** as a control group.

The diet encouraged in the lifestyle change group was largely a whole foods, plant-based **regimen** of fruit, vegetables, whole grains and **legumes**, with few **refined carbohydrates**, Ornish said. It wasn't strictly vegetarian or **vegan**.

"Most people want to feel free, and as soon as you tell someone, 'Don't ever eat this, always eat that,' that's hard to sustain," Ornish said. "If you **indulge** yourself one day, just eat healthier the next."

In addition to changes in diet, the program included 30 minutes of walking six days a week; 60 minutes of daily stress management, mostly in the form of yoga and meditation; and a 60-minute support group session once a week.

Telomere length increased among the men in the lifestyle-intervention group and decreased in the control group. As telomeres become shorter, cells age and die more quickly. The study authors said they are "rather like the tips of shoelaces that keep them from **fraying**."

The study is limited by the small size and by the fact that it wasn't **randomized**, which increases the possibility of unknown sources of bias, the authors said. The results suggest larger randomized studies in different populations would be useful, they said.

(*The Japan Times*, September 17, 2013)

Summarizing the Article Summarize the article below. ニュース記事を以下に要約しましょう。

Comprehensive lifestyle changes were shown to (1) _____ at the cellular level in a study published in the Lancet medical journal. Adopting a diet with more unprocessed foods, combined with (2) _____, increased the length of telomeres, the ends of chromosomes linked to aging. The diet encouraged in the lifestyle change group was largely a whole foods, plant-based regimen of fruit, vegetables, whole grains and legumes, with (3) _____.
In addition to changes in diet, the program included walking, yoga and meditation.

Role Play With your partner, take turns playing the roles of Sam and Chris. パートナーと一緒に、Sam と Chris の役を演じましょう。

☞ In (1), tell Sam a good way to ease tension.
(1) では Sam に、緊張を和らげる方法を教えてあげましょう。

☞ In (2), tell Chris what you think about his idea. You can refer to Useful Expressions.
(2) では Chris のアイデアについてどう思うかを述べましょう。Useful Expressions を使ってもよいです。

[Right before Sam's presentation]

Chris: Are you ready for the presentation, Sam?

Sam: No. I don't think I can make it. I have butterflies in my stomach*.

Chris: Don't worry. You'll be fine.

Sam: But there are so many people out there in the class! What do you do if you get nervous?

Chris: (1)_____.

Sam: (2)_____.
Thanks a lot. I'll do my best.

*have butterflies in one's stomach: to feel very nervous before doing something

---

💬 Useful Expressions

- It sounds ~
- It sounds like ~
- Really? I've never tried it.
- I wonder if that will work.
- I'll give it a shot.

Discussion & Presentation This is a survey conducted on 200 Japanese university students. Work in a group and discuss the questions below. 次のデータは 200 人の日本人大学生に対して行った調査の結果です。グループで以下の質問について話し合いましょう。

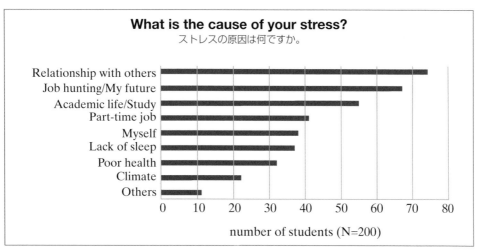

Source: 東海大学新聞

Question What is the cause of your stress? How do you release it? あなたのストレスの原因は何ですか。どのようにしてそのストレスを軽減しますか。

By Yourself Think of your stress and come up with a way to relieve it. 自分のストレスについて考えて、それを緩和する方法を考えましょう。

My stress	How to ease it
e.g., school work	e.g., take a trip

In Your Group Discuss your ideas with your group. Someone in the group should write down all the ideas and opinions. グループ内で自分の考えを発表しましょう。グループ内の一人が全員の考えや意見をメモします。

With the Whole Class Share your group's ideas with the whole class. グループの考えをクラス全体に発表しましょう。

Name	Stress	How to ease it

Culture, Education

Part A: 国連ニュースを読む

―文化・教育―

グローバル化が進む今の時代において、国連は「言語の多様性」について どう考えているのだろうか。

Warm-up Look at the picture and ask your partner, "What do you think about English as an international language?" 写真を見て、パートナーに「国際語としての英語についてどう考えますか」と質問してみましょう。

Vocabulary Match each keyword with its definition. キーワードと意味を結びつけましょう。

(1) linguistic
(2) diversity
(3) preservation
(4) transmission
(5) norm

- (A) when something is kept in its original state or in good condition
- (B) the usual or normal situation, way of doing something
- (C) the fact of including many different types of people or things
- (D) related to language or words
- (E) the process of sending or passing something from one person, place, thing to another

Dialogue Listen to the dialogue. Circle (T) if the statement is true or (F) if it is false. 2人の対話を聞き、内容に合っていれば (T)、違っていれば (F) に○をつけましょう。

(1) Sheryl sometimes talks to Eddie in Filipino. (T) / (F)
(2) People in the Philippines are encouraged to speak English. (T) / (F)
(3) Sheryl's family can all speak multiple languages. (T) / (F)

Reading a News Article With the questions below in mind, read the news article. 先に質問内容に目を通してから、記事を読みましょう。

(1) How many languages are currently spoken around the world?
(2) What did the UN Assembly encourage its member countries to do in 2007?
(3) What did Ms. Bokova say about the prospect of the world's local languages?

On International Day, UN urges support for "Mother Languages," linguistic diversity

国際母語デーで、国連が「母語」と言語の多様性への支持を呼び掛け

21 February 2014 – International Mother Language Day celebrates linguistic and cultural diversity **alongside multilingualism** as a **force** for peace and sustainable development, United Nations officials said today, marking the **commemoration** by calling on countries to promote and protect local languages, "which are keys to global citizenship and **authentic** mutual understanding."

"Recognizing local languages enables more people to make their voices heard and take an active part in their collective fate," said Irina Bokova, Director-General of the UN Educational, Cultural and Scientific Organization (UNESCO), which in its work promotes the harmonious **coexistence** of the 7,000 languages spoken worldwide.

The International Day was **proclaimed** by the UNESCO General Conference in 1999. In 2007, the UN General Assembly adopted a **resolution** calling on Member States "to promote the preservation and protection of all languages used by peoples of the world." By the same text, the Assembly proclaimed 2008 as the International Year of Languages, to promote unity in diversity and international understanding, through multilingualism and multiculturalism.

The 2014 International Day, on the theme "Local languages for global citizenship: spotlight on science," shows how languages ensure access to knowledge, its transmission and its **plurality**. "Contrary to popular wisdom, local languages are perfectly capable of transmitting the most modern scientific knowledge in mathematics, physics, technology, and so on," said Ms. Bokova in her message.

"Recognizing these languages also means opening the door to a great deal of often overlooked traditional scientific knowledge to enrich our overall knowledge base," she continued, adding that local languages **constitute** the majority of languages spoken worldwide in the field of science. They are also the most endangered.

"Excluding languages means excluding those who speak them from their fundamental human right to scientific knowledge," Ms. Bokova said, stressing that in today's "global village" the norm is to use at least three languages, including one local language, one language of wider communication and one international language to communicate at both the local and global levels.

"This linguistic and cultural diversity may be our best chance for the future: for creativity, innovation and **inclusion**. We must not **squander** it," she declared.

(UN News Centre, 21 February, 2014)

Reading Data Look at the data closely and fill in the blanks in the summary.
データをよく見て、要約の穴埋めをしましょう。

Distribution of languages by number of first-language speakers
母語話者数による言語の分布

Population range	Living Languages		Number of speakers	
	Count	Percent	Count	Percent
100,000,000 to 999,999,999	8	0.1%	2,308,548,848	38.7%
10,000,000 to 99,999,999	77	1.1%	2,346,900,757	39.4%
1,000,000 to 9,999,999	304	4.4%	951,916,458	16.0%
100,000 to 999,999	895	13.0%	283,116,716	4.8%
10,000 to 99,999	1,824	26.4%	60,780,797	1.0%
1,000 to 9,999	2,014	29.2%	7,773,810	0.1%
100 to 999	1,038	15.0%	461,250	0.0%
10 to 99	339	4.9%	12,560	0.0%
1 to 9	133	1.9%	521	0.0%
Unknown	277	4.0%		
Totals	6,909		5,959,511,717	

Source: Lewis, M. Paul (ed.), 2009. *Ethnologue: Languages of the World*, Sixteenth edition. Dallas, Texas: SIL International. Online version: http://www.ethnologue.com/16.

The table shows there are (1)_____ languages spoken in the world. Of them, most languages, except the 5.6 percent most popular ones, have fewer than (2)_____ speakers. Also, more than half the languages, 3,838 (55.6 percent,) are used by a small number of people, whose population ranges from (3)_____ to (4)_____. Looking at the number of speakers of those minority languages, it can be pointed out that 94.4 percent of the world's languages are spoken by as little as (5)_____ percent of the world population of approximately (6)_____ billion. On the other hand, only a few languages, (7)_____ (1.2 percent,) are spoken by a large number of about 4.7 billion people (nearly (8)_____ percent.) Another research finding shows that approximately 60 to 80 percent of the world's languages could become extinct in 100 years.

Critical Analysis of Data Examine the pie chart and express your opinion in My opinions & ideas. 円グラフを見て My opinions & ideas に自分の意見を記入しましょう。

World languages by degree of vitality
世界の言語の存続度合い

- Safe or data-deficient
- Vulnerable (not spoken by children outside the home)
- Definitely endangered (children not speaking)
- Severely endangered (only spoken by the oldest generations)
- Critically endangered (spoken by few members of the oldest generation)
- Extinct since 1950

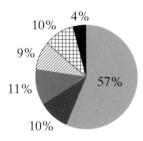

Source: the Atlas of the World's Languages in Danger, 2010. ©UNESCO
Note: Details may not add up to total shown because of rounding.

Why are many languages not likely to be spoken in the world? I think there are a number of reasons behind it. One is (1) _____
_____.
Another reason is (2) _____
_____.
    (3) _____ is an extinct language that I know of. I think endangered languages (4) _____ be protected because (5) _____
_____.

Sharing Your Opinions Share your opinions and ideas in your group. Write anything you find interesting about others' ideas. グループ内で自分の意見や考えについて話し合いましょう。面白いと思った他の人の意見を書きましょう。

Culture, Education

Part B: The Japan Times を読む

―文化・教育―

「英語以外の教科も英語で！」という議論に沸き立つフランス。その政策の背景と実施された場合の影響について考えてみよう。

Listening and Taking Notes Listen to the first part of a news article. You can take notes while listening. ニュース記事の前半を聞きましょう。聞きながらメモをしてもよいです。

Notes

Understanding a News Article Skim the article while referring to the Glossary. 巻末の用語集を参照しつつ、記事をざっと読んで概要を把握しましょう。

English-language education proposal has French up in arms

英語教育提案に身構えるフランス人

PARIS – There was a time, not so long ago, when anyone with a proper education spoke French. Diplomacy and business were conducted in French. Knowledge was spread in French. Travelers made their way in French and, of course, lovers traded **sweet nothings** in French.

Viewed from France, the trouble with modern times is that many of those activities are now conducted in English, even by the French. In a country that cares so much about its language it maintains a whole ministry to promote it, that alone is enough to stir passionate debate in Paris.

But there is more.

Higher Education Minister Genevieve Fioraso last week introduced a bill that will allow French universities to teach more courses in English, even when English is not the subject. The goal, she explained, is to attract more students from such countries as China, Brazil and India, where English is widely taught but French is reserved largely for literature lovers.

"Ten years ago, we were third in welcoming foreign students, but today we are fifth," she said in a Q&A in the magazine *Nouvel Observateur*. "Why have we lost so much attraction? Because Germany has put in place an English program that has passed us by. We must make up the gap."

The idea proposed by Fioraso, herself a former English and economics teacher, sounds **patriotic** enough. Yet it has sparked cultural and nationalist **outrage**—not only from Paris **intellectuals**, but also from several dozen members of Parliament— opposition as well as Socialist—who insist that learning French should be part of any foreign student's experience in France.

The controversy flows from the same **wellspring** as France's effort to maintain foreign barriers and cultural subsidies despite the U.S.-European free trade negotiations presently **getting under way**. Without government help in limiting imports and financing local artists, it is feared, French culture will soon be **swamped** by a tsunami of American products.

Culture Minister Aurelie Filippetti last week persuaded 13 of her EU **counterparts** to join her in an appeal for cultural protections to be excluded from the talks, preserving what the French call "the cultural exception."

Member states "would be **compromised**" if the subsidies and **quotas** were not assured, they warned.

(*The Japan Times*, May 20, 2013)

Summarizing the Article Summarize the article below. ニュース記事を以下に要約しましょう。

PARIS – Formerly, French was the "international language," used for business, diplomacy and travel. Recently, (1) _____, which troubles some in France. Last week, a bill was introduced to allow (2) _____, the goal being to attract more international students. This proposal has sparked outrage, from intellectuals to members of Parliament. The controversy is related to concerns about cultural protections in light of the current (3) _____. They fear that without protections, their culture will be compromised.

Role Play With your partner, take turns playing the roles of Sam and Chris. パートナーと一緒に、Sam と Chris の役を演じましょう。

☞ In (1), tell Sam whether their university should have classes all taught in English.
(1) では Sam に、自分たちの大学の授業が全て英語で行われるべきかどうかを述べましょう。

☞ In (2), tell Chris what you think about Chris's idea. You can refer to Useful Expressions.
(2) では Chris のアイデアについてどう思うかを述べましょう。Useful Expressions を使ってもよいです。

[Chris and Sam talk about English education in Japan.]

Chris: Now it seems drastic changes are being made for English education in Japan.

Sam: Yes. In high school, English has to be taught in English, basically. And the government panel once suggested TOEFL be used as an entrance exam.

Chris: Some universities have even made it mandatory to teach all courses in English.

Sam: I know, but I'm not sure about these changes. What if our university followed suit?

Chris: (1)_____.

Sam: (2)_____.

💬 Useful Expressions

- I couldn't agree more.
- I see.
- That doesn't seem possible.
- That's interesting.
- I still don't get it.
- I'm skeptical about it.

Discussion & Presentation This is a graph on the percentage of international students from Japan, China India, and Korea in U.S. universities. Work in a group and discuss the question below. 次のデータは米国大学における日本・中国・インド・韓国の留学生の割合についてのグラフです。グループで以下の質問について話し合いましょう。

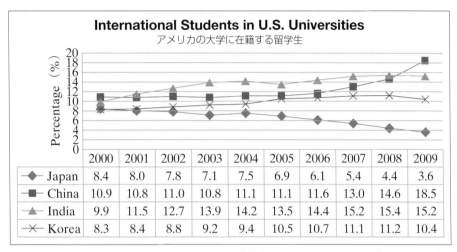

Source: 産学官によるグローバル人材の育成のための戦略

Question What can Japan do to develop global human resources? 日本はグローバル人材を育成するために何ができますか。

By Yourself Think of a strategy to develop global human resources. グローバル人材を育成する戦略について考えましょう。

Field	How to develop it
e.g., language	e.g., enhance English skills for study abroad

In Your Group Discuss your ideas with your group. Someone in the group should write down all the ideas and opinions. グループ内で自分の考えを発表しましょう。グループ内の一人が全員の考えや意見をメモします。

With the Whole Class Share your group's ideas with the whole class. グループの考えをクラス全体に発表しましょう。

Name	Field	How to develop it

Glossary

Unit 1
Part A
routinely　日常的に
subjected to ~　~にさらされる、~の標的となる
indiscriminate brutality　無差別な残虐行為
sombrely（＝somberly）　厳粛に
regime　体制、制度
take steps　対策を講じる
feasible　実行可能な
impunity　処罰を受けないこと、免責
violations　違反、妨害、違反行為
abuse of human rights　人権侵害
rotating presidency　輪番議長（制）
genocide　大規模な虐殺
(be) mandated to ~　~の権限を与えられる
implementation　遂行

Part B
air raid　空襲、空爆
presumably　おそらく
flee　逃げる
oral history　口述歴史、口承による言い伝え
validate　立証する
testimony　証言
ledger　帳簿、名簿
age bracket　年齢層
incendiary bomb　焼夷（しょうい）弾
death toll　死亡者数

Unit 2
Part A
address　取り組む
cripple　損なう

staggering　驚くほどの
outflow　流出
inaugurate　始動させる
debilitating　消耗させるような
distinguished　著名な
narcotic　麻薬、薬物
human trafficking　人身売買

Part B
in (one's) cross hairs for　~に照準を合わせている、ターゲットにしている
roasting　厳しい批判
expedite　迅速に処理する
royalty payment　（ブランドなどの）使用料
grapple with~　~に取り組む
austerity　緊縮財政
obligation　義務、責任

Unit 3
Part A
daunting　気が遠くなる
secure　確保する
sweep　押し寄せる
displace　（人を）退去させる
destroy　~を破壊する
livelihood　生計、暮らし
resilience　回復力
bear the brunt of ~　~の矢面に立つ
fury　猛威
appeal　要請
pledge　寄付金
hamper　妨げる

Part B

resume　再開する
clear up　解決する
kidnap　拉致する
take office　就任する
draw a parallel　比較する
regime　政権
relent on ~　~を諦める
resolution　決意
abduct　拉致する
gross　非常な
perpetrator　加害者
rapporteur　報告担当者

Unit 4
Part A

envoy　大使
galvanize　活性化する
stakeholder　利害関係者
mobilize　結集する
implement　実行する
sustainable　持続可能な
bold　大胆な
robust　頑健な
strain　負荷
institute　制定する
water main　水道本管
mass transit　大量輸送
congestion　混雑

Part B

mandatory　義務的な
trigger　きっかけとなる
curb　制限
large-lot　大口の
cap-and-trade　排出量取引

trim　減らす
stringent　厳しい
consecutive　連続した
slash　削減する
amount to ~　合計~になる
retain　保持する

Unit 5
Part A

elicit　引き起こす
crimes against humanity　人道に対する罪
humanitarian　人道的な
gravity　重大さ
parallel　類似点
population　人口
rectify　是正する

Part B

assassination　暗殺
deprive A of B　AからBを奪う
plight　苦境、窮状
suppress　抑圧する
enchain　鎖でつなぐ、制限する
acclaim　称賛
hypocrisy　偽善（行為）
drone　無人機
autobiography　自伝
dire　恐ろしい、ものすごい、ひどい

Unit 6
Part A

policy-making　政策立案
sustainable　持続可能な、環境に優しい
eradicate　撲滅させる
inaugural meeting　設立の総会
eminent　著名な

discipline 領域、分野
geologic epoch 地質学的な時代
tackle 取り組む、対処する
urbanization 都市化現象
sanitation 公衆衛生
catalyse 触媒する、促進させる
agenda 計画、指針
highlight 強調する
disarmament 軍備縮小、軍縮

Part B
create a stir 物議を醸す
radioactive 放射能の
contradict 反論する、否定する
contaminated 汚染された
reportedly 伝えられるところによると
compound 敷地
contaminant 汚染物質
reactor 原子炉

Unit 7
Part A
lay the groundwork 下準備をする
empower 権利を与える
photo-op 写真撮影時間
crucial 極めて重要な
the Millennium Development Goals ミレニアム開発目標（= MDGs）
landmark 歴史的な、重要な
The Beijing Declaration and the Platform for Action 北京宣言及び行動綱領
unanimously 満場一致で
sexual orientation 性的指向
showcase 紹介する、披露する
on the margins of ~ ~の合間に
biodiversity 種（しゅ）の多様性

Part B
jolt 揺さぶりをかける
economic coma 景気低迷
shrink 減少する
plummet 急落する
implore 要請する
abortion 妊娠中絶
boardroom 役員室
recession 景気後退
stagnation 景気停滞
uniform 画一的な
womenomics ウーマノミクス（女性が創出する経済）
go off-ramp 車線から出口に向かう

Unit 8
Part A
ethical 倫理的な、道徳的な
repercussion 影響、波紋
proceed 利益
recourse 助けを求めて頼る人やもの
faulty 欠陥のある
antihistamine 抗ヒスタミン薬
smuggling 密輸

Part B
opium アヘン
wean off~ ~を止めさせる
narcotic 麻薬、薬物
poppy ケシ、ポピー、ケシ色
tried and true 絶対確実な、実証済みの
insurgent 暴徒、反乱者
backfire 裏目に出る、思わぬ面倒な事態を招く
addiction 中毒
tangible 具体的な、明らかな

Unit 9
Part A

diabetes　糖尿病
world of plenty　（物質的に）豊かな世界
smallholder　小農家
produce　農作物
projection　見通し、予測
obesity　肥満
non-communicable disease　非伝染性疾病
pancreas　膵臓（すいぞう）
insulin　インシュリン
premature illness　若年性疾患
cardiovascular disease　循環器疾患
diagnosis　診断
instrumental　役立つ、貢献する

Part B

meditation　瞑想（めいそう）
cellular　細胞の
telomere　染色体末端部位、テロメア
chromosome　染色体
preventive medicine　予防医学
coronary　冠状動脈の
reimburse　補償する
immortality enzyme　不死の酵素
autism　自閉症
prostate cancer　前立腺がん
surveillance　監視
regimen　食事療法
legume　豆類
refined carbohydrate　精製炭水化物
vegan　完全菜食主義者（卵や乳製品などの摂取も避ける人）
indulge　甘やかす
fray　擦り切れる
randomize　無作為抽出する

Unit 10
Part A

alongside ~　~と共に
multilingualism　多言語主義
force　原動力
commemoration　記念
authentic　真の
coexistence　共存
proclaim　宣言する
resolution　決議
plurality　多元性
constitute　占める
inclusion　一体化
squander　逸する

Part B

sweet nothing　愛の言葉
patriotic　愛国的な
outrage　怒り
intellectual　有識者
wellspring　水源
get under way　始まる
swamp　水没させる
counterpart　対応する相手
compromise　妥協する
quota　割り当て

編　者
　　　日本国際連合協会　　（にほんこくさいれんごうきょうかい）
編著者
　　　武藤　克彦　　（むとう　かつひこ）
　　　石渡　淳元　　（いしわた　あつもと）
　　　長　　和重　　（ちょう　かずしげ）
　　　James Francis　（ジェイムズ・フランシス）
　　　仲　　慶次　　（なか　けいじ）
編集協力
　　　服部　孝彦　　（はっとり　たかひこ）
　　　池田　真　　　（いけだ　まこと）

国際情勢を考える─国連ニュースで読む世界

2015 年 2 月 20 日　第 1 版発行
2023 年 3 月 20 日　第 6 版発行

編著者──武藤克彦／石渡淳元／長　和重／James Francis／仲　慶次
発行者──前田俊秀
発行所──株式会社三修社
　　　　〒150-0001　東京都渋谷区神宮前 2-2-22
　　　　TEL 03-3405-4511 ／ FAX 03-3405-4522
　　　　https://www.sanshusha.co.jp
　　　　振替 00190-9-72758
印刷所──倉敷印刷株式会社

©2015 Printed in Japan　ISBN978-4-384-33450-0　C1082
表紙デザイン──土橋公政
準拠 CD 録音──一般財団法人 英語教育協議会（ELEC）
準拠 CD 製作──高速録音株式会社
編集──山本　拓

JCOPY〈出版者著作権管理機構　委託出版物〉
本書の無断複製は著作権法上での例外を除き禁じられています。複製される場合は、
そのつど事前に、出版者著作権管理機構（電話 03-5244-5088 FAX 03-5244-5089
e-mail: info@jcopy.or.jp）の許諾を得てください。

教科書準拠 CD 発売
本書の準拠 CD をご希望の方は弊社までお問い合わせください。